Wyoming Hiking Trails

Wyoming Hiking Trails

The Salt River, Wyoming, Gros Ventre, and Wind River Ranges

By Tom and Sanse Sudduth

PRUETT PUBLISHING COMPANY
Boulder, Colorado 80301

Contents

KEY MAP

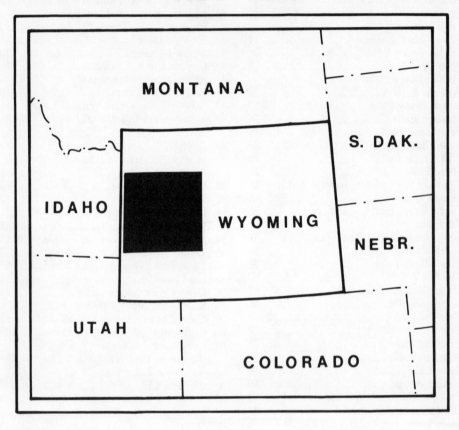

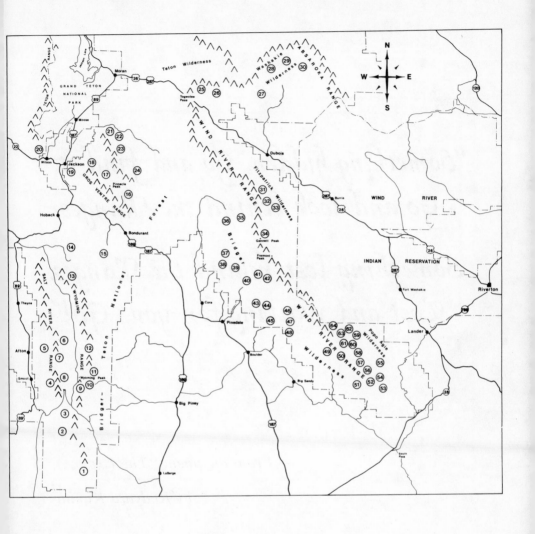

Legend

Starting Point	●
Trail	− − − − −
Alternate Route	− − →
Mileage	9.0
Stopping Point	⬡

"Something hidden. Go and find it.
  Go and look behind the Ranges—

Something lost behind the Ranges.
  Lost and waiting for you. Go!"

— From the poem "The Explorer"

by Rudyard Kipling

INTRODUCTION

Picture the Wyoming mountains in early summer. Tangy sage spices the cool morning air and a heavy dew drips from the grasses in the meadows. Across the valley a doe trots into the aspen, leading her still-spotted twin fawns. All is whisper-quiet until a beaver slaps his tail on a nearby pond and dives. At midday the warming sun promotes the spring break-up on higher slopes. Snow melt washes the rocky tundra; swollen, rushing streams carry small ice floes; a rich smell of earth permeates the air. The magical change of seasons takes place, a dazzling performance in the midst of solitude, unwatched, eternal. Early summer, a nice time to visit the Wyoming mountains.

But consider the lofty peaks and winding valleys of Wyoming's high country in mid-summer. Hot sun and afternoon showers bring a sudden flourish of color to the landscape. Delicate, sky-blue flax line the trails, reds of various paintbrush accent the sage, and other wildflowers of yellow, violet, deep purple, and rose bloom across the hillsides. In the early mornings and late afternoons trout rise on the mountain lakes, sending rippling rings across the water. Everywhere there is wildlife: moose in the willowed valleys, squirrels, chipmunks, marmots in the conifer-covered hillsides, ducks in the rivers and on the ponds. And day after day of sunshine and blue sky which create ideal camping conditions. Ah, summertime in Wyoming!

Think, however, of the magnificent autumn in the Wyoming ranges. By some regal authority the usual Labor Day snow pronounces an end to all bothersome mosquitoes and fair weather tourists. And then Indian summer follows. In mornings and evenings the air has a frosty nip, but at midday the mountain lands fairly glow with a melancholy warmth. Groves of rustling aspen blaze bright yellow with the sunlight and many shrubs and ferns turn rich colors of red and gold. Buck deer now display hard rather than velveted antlers, and bull elk in rut serenade with high-pitched bugles at night. And soon new snow begins to dust the highest peaks, the harbinger of yet another winter.

When is the best time to visit the high Wyoming ranges? Early summer, mid-summer, fall, even winter, each season offers distinctive rewards to the hiker and backpacker and each requires special preparation. The change of seasons during early summer and fall is a magical, exciting performance not to be missed, but muddy access roads and trails and large snowbanks at higher elevations must be reckoned with. The Wyoming summer with its beautiful weather attracts an ever-growing number of outdoorsmen so trails must be chosen carefully to avoid the crowds. Deep snows and bitter winds of winter require the most extensive preparation for a backpack trip but more and more winter campers are venturing into the backcountry, seeking the solitude and discovering the exquisite beauty of the ice-and-snow landscape. But of course the best time for a backpack trip in Wyoming is any time it can be fit into your schedule, the sooner the better. Rudyard Kipling in his poem "The Explorer" wrote of the wilderness call, of "a voice, as bad as Conscience" which repeated "On one everlasting Whisper day and night":

"Something hidden. Go and find it. Go and look behind
   the Ranges —
"Something lost behind the Ranges. Lost and waiting
   for you. Go!

The authors through this book invite you to the ranges also.

SALT RIVER RANGE. Of the four main Wyoming ranges described in this guide, the Salt River Range and the Wyoming Range, which form the west half of the Bridger National Forests, are the least known and least explored. The sharp, 10,000-foot peaks of the Salt River Range crest into the skyline high above the Star Valley and Idaho border (west) and the Greys River Valley (east). Rock Lake Peak at 10,770 feet marks its highest point, and several glacier-carved lakes and tarns, barren of fish but with stunning alpine scenery, dot its crest. Trail construction and maintenance in this region, as well as in the Wyoming Range, receive less priority than other Forest Service interests, in contrast to the Gros Ventre and Wind River Ranges. But the lack of bridges at stream crossings, corduroy paths across marshes, signs at every junction, and other trail refinements emphasize the feeling that this is true wilderness. While literally thousands of hikers and backpackers will enter the Wind River Range on a typical Fourth of July weekend, the combined total for both the Salt River and Wyoming Ranges will be a few hundred, concentrated mostly in the campgrounds. The key in sorting out the trails and in discovering new places to explore is the new U.S.G.S. topographic maps, available now (and included in this book) as one-color advance proofs. The final editions of these maps will be published beginning in 1979. Unfortunately, the Salt River Range lacks protection under the National Wilderness Preservation System and although the bulk of the mountains have been preserved through simple lack of exposure and use, jeep roads and motor bike trails tear away more every year at the edges. In recent years the suspected presence of oil deposits in the Overthrust Belt beneath this range has encouraged exploration, and drilling may begin as soon as 1978.

WYOMING RANGE. These massive mountains, rounded and covered with snow patches through July, form a sister range to the Salt River Range and rise between the Greys River Valley (west) and the great Wyoming Basin (east). From 11,380-foot Wyoming Peak — the highest point in the range — the view encompasses the wavy length of the Salt River Range west and extends toward the flat-topped Commissary Ridge southwest. The rolling humps of the rest of the Wyoming Range show north, continuing toward the Hoback River, and even distant sharp spires of the Wind River Range can be seen east across the Wyoming Basin. As with the Salt River Range, the prime virtues for the hiker and backpacker here are the abundant wildlife and, as yet, the solitude. Stands of spruce, fir, and pine fill the sub-alpine slopes; fragile rock-and-grass tundra covers the high peaktops; crystal-clear creeks and magnificent cascades and waterfalls greatly outnumber the few lakes. Although some permits are issued for timber harvest on the lower slopes, there is usually no cutting above 9,500 feet in elevation. In general, the Wyoming Range offers better one- and two-day trips to places of uncrowded wilderness than do the Gros Ventre and Wind River Ranges. But again, trail finding can be difficult and the new U.S.G.S. topographic maps are needed to stay on course. Several U.S.G.S. advance proof topographic maps were used for the map photos in this book; the final maps will be published on the same schedule as those for the Salt River Range. A main trail for one- and two-week trips through the Wyoming Range is the Wyoming Range Trail which begins near Snider Basin at the south end and traverses the east slope to the McDougal Gap Road toward the north end, linking other trails described as one-day trips. With a supply pick-up at McDougal Gap, the trip can be extended through the Hoback Mountains on various trails to the Hoback River.

GROS VENTRE RANGE. The name "Gros Ventre" (pronounced Grow VAHNT) translates from French as "Big Bellies" and was used by French trappers to describe the band of Arapaho Indians who occasionally traveled through the west-central Wyoming mountains. Perhaps the name originated because the Arapahoes would ask for food from the trappers, signifying their hunger in common sign language by passing their hand in front of their stomach. The Gros Ventre Range forms part of the eastern boundary of Jackson Hole and continues from northwest to southeast, roughly at a right angle to the Teton Range on the west side of Jackson Hole. These gray, rounded summits, shaped from sedimentary deposits and uplifted about 50 million years ago, contrast distinctly with the ragged, geologically-young Tetons. The highest point is Doubletop Peak, listed at 11,682 feet by the U.S. Geological Survey and at 11,750 feet by the Forest Service. Eight peaks rise above 11,000 feet and dozens crest over 10,000 feet. Although many of the trails from the Gros Ventre River begin in dry sagebrush country, they soon climb into scenic forests of aspen, lodgepole and whitebark pine, Engelmann spruce, and alpine fir. These trails carry less traffic than those which begin closer to the town of Jackson and along the Hoback River. Currently, a South Gros Ventre Planning Unit has been formed to study this range for possible inclusion in the Wilderness System. The Wilderness Proposal will be sent to Congress in December 1979.

WIND RIVER RANGE. Wyoming's famous Wind River Range forms the eastern flange of the horseshoe-shaped Bridger-Teton National Forest. The range begins near Togwotee Pass through which U.S. 26/287 runs, bears southeast forming the high Continental Divide between the Wyoming Basin (southwest) and the Wind River Valley and Wind River Indian Reservation (northeast), and dissolves into foothills after some 80 miles around South Pass. Of the many jagged, granite-and-ice peaks in this spectacular region which rise over 13,000 feet, Gannett Peak at 13,785 feet tops them all, the highest point in Wyoming. And beneath the peaktops many glaciers, remnants of the last Ice Age, cling to the high alpine slopes, including the seven largest in the United States outside of Alaska.

Most of the Wind River Range has been (or soon will be) incorporated into the National Wilderness Preservation System. The Fitzpatrick Wilderness, at the north end of the range south of Dubois (pronounced DO Boys), was formed by Congress in 1976 from the existing Glacier Primitive Area. The name memorializes mountainman/fur trader Thomas Fitzpatrick who explored much of the Wind River Range and was a partner in the Rocky Mountain Fur Company with Jim Bridger, after whom the nearby Bridger Wilderness was named. This is a region of "Shining Mountains," high mounds of granite so polished by glaciers that they gleam in the afternoon sun. It contains scores of high mountain lakes, many still unnamed, which lie in glacier-gouged pockets beneath the crest of the range west. A flock of bighorn sheep inhabits Whiskey Mountain and the surrounding hills; moose, elk, mule deer and black bear range throughout the thirty-mile-long Wilderness area. Since the closing of the Wind River Indian Reservation to backpackers in 1974 (see below), the Glacier Trail from the Torrey Creek Entrance has provided the main access into the heart of the Fitzpatrick. This long, north-south trail is recommended for eight- and ten-day trips.

The popular Bridger Wilderness runs the length of the west side of the Wind River Range and contains over 380,000 acres. Long a national outdoor recreation area, these towering mountains and deep forests were designated by the Forest Service as a Primitive Area in 1931 and received into the Wilderness System in 1964, the year the Wilderness Act was passed by Congress. As with the Fitzpatrick and Popo Agie Wildernesses, the Bridger is covered with shimmering lakes and tarns—over 1,300 in all—which at lower elevations support populations of brook, brown, cutthroat, golden, mackinaw, and rainbow trout and other game fish. A main blessing-and-curse of this long, narrow Wilderness is its easy access, a joy for the backpacker who wants to get quickly into the middle of the range but a main factor in the popularity, and hence, over-use of the Bridger. The five primary entrances of Green River Lakes, New Fork Lake, Elkhart Park, Boulder Lake, and Big Sandy Lake provide very accessible take-off points, making extended trips from one entrance to another easy. But these primary entrances suffer from heavy over-use in July and August and, for the true lover of solitude and serenity, are not recommended for those months. The five secondary entrances of Willow Creek, Upper Half Moon Campground, Little Half Moon Lake, Scab Creek, and Sweetwater listed in this book, although not so elaborately developed, make better starting points during summer. Over 500 miles of maintained trails link the entrances and thread through the valleys and mountains for the 80 mile length of the Bridger Wilderness. Special trail maps can be purchased from the Ranger District office in Pinedale, which are adequate for most trips. However, they lack the fine detail and topographic information available on the U.S.G.S. topographic maps.

The Popo Agie (pronounced Po POZ yuh) Primitive Area rounds out the southeast end of the Wind River Range, west of Lander and south of the Wind River Indian Reservation. Its name originates from the language of the Crow Indian and translates as "headwaters," referring to the sources of the Popo Agie River which drain this spectacular region. The Forest Service established the Popo Agie Primitive Area in 1932 and recommended it for Wilderness designation in 1974. Although three different boundaries are being studied before a final determination is made, it appears certain that the bulk of these mountains will be protected soon within the Wilderness System. Thus, the text refers to the "Popo Agie Wilderness" elsewhere in this book. High, jagged peaks, sheer cliff walls, and narrow valleys and canyons characterize this 24 mile stretch of the "Winds." Many of the twenty summits above 12,000 feet display their most rugged, awesome face on this northeast side of the range rather than on the southwest or Bridger Wilderness side. Of the 240-plus lakes which cover the landscape, 46 provide ideal aquatic habitat which now support fish, managed carefully by the Wyoming Game and Fish Department. Access is currently limited to three main trailheads: The Sweetwater Entrance in the Bridger Wilderness at the south end of the range, the Deer Park Entrance north of Worthen Meadow Reservoir near the middle, and, most popular, the Dickinson Park Entrance at the north end.

WIND RIVER INDIAN RESERVATION. This private, square-shaped reserve, owned by the Shoshone and Arapahoe Tribes, comprises over two million acres east of Dubois and north of Lander. Its southwest corner includes the Wind River Range as far as the Continental Divide and separates the Fitzpatrick Wilderness from the Popo Agie Wilderness. In the past the Joint Business Council of the Tribes did allow non-Indians to backpack on the Reservation but since 1974 this policy has been discontinued. Access is no longer permitted from the St. Lawrence Basin Entrance on the St. Lawrence Creek, South Fork, and North Fork of the Little Wind River Trails nor from the Burris Entrance on the Ink Wells Trail. It is very doubtful that the Reservation will be opened for backpacking any time in the near future. For the most recent information, write: Joint Business Council, Shoshone and Arapahoe Tribes, Box 217, Fort Washakie, Wyoming 82514.

HOW TO USE THIS BOOK

Each hike in this book is presented with an information capsule, a text of information, a scenic photo or two, and a photo of the relevant United States Geological Survey topographic map.

The information capsule preceding the text summarizes the hike in ten important facts and allows a means for quick comparison with other hikes.

First, each hike is recommended as a **half-day trip, one day trip** or **backpack** depending on the distance, type of terrain, and possible destinations. Half-day trips usually measure 2 miles or less one way and one day trips figure at most between 6 and 7 miles one way. These trips can be done with a day pack only, with lunch, appropriate extra clothing, and equipment for an emergency bivouac. Trips classified as one day *or* backpack can be done safely in one (but sometimes long) day with a light pack and an early start. Or, because of length, possible sidetrips, or a very scenic and exciting destination, they might be attempted in two more days, with a larger pack of overnight provisions and, hence, at a slower pace. Backpack trips reach a suggested point too far into the backcountry to allow a safe return in the same day and require sleeping bag, tent or ground cover, cooking utensils and food.

Hiking **distance,** given in both miles and kilometers, is measured carefully one way only and rounded to the nearest tenth of a mile. Some Forest Service mileage signs round distances to the nearest mile or half-mile, others give estimated or outdated distances. Thus, the posted figures will not always agree with those recorded in this book. *Where distances to more than one point or destination are listed, the elevation gain and loss and maximum elevation (see below) are determined from the last listed destination.*

Hiking time is given as a guide only for those who are not sure of their pace. It is determined from a basic rate of 1½ miles per hour and then adjusted for the roughness of the terrain, steepness of the grade and total elevation gain. Driving time and rest and lunch stops are not included.

Elevation gain and **loss,** figured in both feet and meters, measures the total accumulated climb and drop of the hike, not just the difference between the lowest and highest point. More than any other factor, the elevation gain determines the difficulty of the trail. The greater the gain, the more the time, strength, and energy is required for the hike.

High elevation contributes to several unique and predictable conditions on any hiking trail. Weather changes very quickly: A snow squall can suddenly blow in, turn into a brief shower of rain, and then evaporate into blue skies and hot sun, all in a single afternoon. In general, with every 1,000-foot rise in elevation wind velocity increases by two or three times and air temperature decreases by 3°C/2°C. At 10,000 feet the amount of oxygen in the air is 31% less than at sea level. Plant life varies considerably with elevation: Blue spruce will seldom be found above 7,000 feet while Engelmann spruce range from 6,800 feet to 10,000 and 12,000 feet. And at timberline (usually around 10,250 feet in central Wyoming) the mountains undergo a remarkable transformation, shedding their protection of scattered tree clumps for the spartan cover of alpine flowers, grasses and twisted, wind-stunted shrubs. Since it is enjoyable to notice these high elevation changes and necessary to prepare for some of them, the **maximum elevation** or highest point of the trail is indicated.

All trails in the National Forests are open to backpackers throughout the year. However, in early summer many access roads become impassable with mud, unbridged rivers are difficult to cross safely, and large snowbanks still blanket the trail. The **season** listed for each hike represents an educated guess by Forest Service rangers and experienced backpackers of those months when the trail will be accessible and free of enough snow for hiking.

All appropriate **U.S.G.S. topographic maps** and their publication dates are listed in the order that the trail crosses them. These maps provide extremely useful information for hiking and backpacking trips, especially for the longer or less obvious trails. Based on aerial photographs, they show the shape and elevation of the terrain, plot major trails, roads, creeks, and lakes, and differentiate between woodland, scrub, and open areas. U.S.G.S. topo maps are available for purchase at most mountaineering shops or may be obtained from the U.S. government by sending the map name and $1.25 per map to the Central Region-Map Distribution, U.S. Geological Survey, Denver Federal Center, Bldg. 41, Denver, Colorado 80225.

And, as final items in the information capsule, the relevant **Ranger District** and **National Forest** are given to help place the tour geographically and to identify a source of further information.

Each text is organized into a paragraph or two of introduction, a paragraph of driving directions, and several paragraphs of specific trail information. The introduction discusses the outstanding features of the hike and points out interesting history and the origin of place names, spectacular viewpoints, and prevalent hazards. For some hikes the particular species of fish, relevant to the lake in the title or as otherwise given, is listed at the end of the paragraph. The paragraph of driving directions gives distances and instructions from the nearest town or landmark to the trailhead. Parking areas and variable road conditions are also mentioned. The remaining paragraphs summarize the tour route and identify the most spectacular vistas, the promising alternate routes and possible trip extensions, and unique trail features.

General directions, such as "east-northeast" and "southwest," are based on true north for landmarks as they appear on the topo map rather than on magnetic north as they would read on a compass. Specific directions, such as "152°/SSE," are given when more accurate orientation is needed, listed first with the exact bearing based on magnetic north, then second with the bearing based on true north (magnetic bearing + approx. 17°) and rounded to the sixteen points of the compass. *To use the magnetic bearing (with a Silva Compass), simply dial the bearing, align the compass needle with the orienting arrow, and look along the direction-of-travel arrowhead.*

All photos in the book were taken by the authors during their field work and were chosen because they represent some highlight or typical scene, or the destination of the hike.

The map photos are enlarged or reduced sections of U.S.G.S. topographic maps onto which the trails and mileages have been drafted. Other symbols that have been drafted onto the maps such as the "starting point" and "alternate route" are listed in the LEGEND. These maps correlate closely with the trail description. *For the best understanding of the hike, read the text and at the same time, follow the trail carefully along the map, noting each prominent feature as described.*

HIKING AND BACKPACKING IN WYOMING

The "how to" of hiking and backpacking is not within the scope of this guidebook. Many other excellent books and magazines provide complete information on this subject. However, a few specific points about conditions within the west-central Wyoming ranges might be pointed out.

TRAVEL HINTS. In June and early July many unbridged streams and rivers — high, and fast and ice-cold from snow melt — become very difficult to ford. Do not hesitate to turn back at these crossings; never take an unreasonable risk. Use a safety rope secured upstream; find natural log bridges; keep your boots on to cross faster and perhaps wear nylon overboots.

Be prepared for the not-too-serious but annoying pests that you might encounter on your trip. Leave no food in your car at the trailhead unless you are certain that it is mouse-tight. Also protect your food cache and deliciously salty boots and pack from rodents at your campsite. In early season pack repellent to foil the attack of mosquitoes and check yourself carefully each night for wood ticks. Larger beasts pose little threat in any of the areas covered in this book. A cow moose might become a little belligerent in an attempt to protect her calf if you should happen to venture too close. But a firearm for protection is unneeded and out-of-place in the wilderness.

The relevant U.S. Geological Survey topographic maps, from which the map photos for this book were taken, make a most useful tool for orientation and route selection. If possible, order the maps from the Central Region-Map Distribution in Denver (see HOW TO USE THIS BOOK), especially for the Salt River and Wyoming Ranges, rather than depend on finding them in the Wyoming towns.

Many hikes in this book travel to elevations of 9,000 and 10,000 feet or higher. If you come from a considerably lower elevation make sure that you give your body a few days to acclimatize. Be alert for symptoms of mountain sickness such as loss of appetite, headache, nausea, and dizziness. Hike at a slow but steady pace, rest frequently, carry a water bottle and take frequent sips to offset dehydration.

WILDLIFE AND FISH

A main delight on any hiking or backpacking trip in west-central Wyoming is the opportunity to observe wildlife. The high mountains and surrounding hills contain a wide variety of mammals and birds, a *de facto* preserve which has been little influenced by man. As they have for thousands of years now, pikas nest in boulder fields on the alpine mountainsides and bark at passing intruders. Red squirrels scamper branch to branch in the lodgepole and limber pine while the tiny least chipmunks hunt for seeds and berries among the rock piles below. Long-legged whitetail jackrabbits are commonly spotted along the sage-lined roads on the drive to the trailhead, as are pronghorn antelope. The largest pronghorn herd in the United States resides in Wyoming; its fleet-footed members reach speeds of 60 miles per hour for short distances and are thought to be the fastest American animal.

Other animals such as the shorttail weasel, mink, marten, river otter, and badger, though wary and less often seen, inhabit the open forest and valley bottoms. Gray fox, red fox, coyote, bobcat, and black bear range throughout these west-central mountains, although the evidence of their presence too is often only a footprint along the trail. The habitat of grizzly bear does not extend as far south as the area covered in this book. (The last confirmed sighting and track of a grizzly in the Wind River Range was in 1976 of an old boar along Soda Creek north of Soda Lake.) But sporadic, unconfirmed sightings of gray wolves indicate the possible reestablishment of these beautiful animals within the Gros Ventre and Wind River Ranges.

.Of the big game animals, the most common and one of the most enjoyable to watch are the

6

moose, spotted often in woodlands around nearby lakes or in valley bottoms of willows. Wide-eared, black-tailed mule deer, also very plentiful, can be seen throughout the sage hills and forested mountains, the buck with velveted antlers in summer. Most intelligent and magnificent of the deer family, the elk or wapiti frequent the lowlands in early spring and roam the higher elevations in the mountains during summer. They flee at the slightest sight or smell of humans and sometimes can be heard from the trail crashing their way through timber. And on the higher mountain slopes above the thicker conifer forests, the famous bighorn sheep find a home, observed best across the wide stretches of tundra with the aid of binoculars. The old rams with massive coiled horns, as featured in many books, are seen less frequently then the ewes and kids.

Bird-watchers will have a wonderful opportunity to identify many different birds in the west-central Wyoming mountains. The ubiquitous Oregon junco flits through conifer forests, flashing the white feathers of his tail. Dippers and kill deers inspect the rocks along the creeks and mallard and pintail ducks nest near the many lakes. The sandhill crane, golden eagle, blue grouse and over 200 other impressive fowl inhabit the mountains.

For the fisherman, the rivers and lakes in the west-central ranges rate as some of the finest fishing waters in the United States. (A fishing license is required, available in most Wyoming towns.) Even the casual observer of fish will enjoy stopping next to a creek for lunch and quietly watching, say, a wily, orange-finned brookie swim steadily into the current and hunt for his dinner. The different specie(s) of fish found in the various lakes of west-central Wyoming are listed in the INDEX. The following paragraphs provide description of some of the most popular Wyoming game fish:

Brook trout (abbreviated in the text and index as Brk): Yellow-green, wormy patterns on back, freckles of red with an outer blue ring along side, colorful orange-red bottom fins.

Brown trout (Brn): Black freckles on upper side, freckles of red with light-blue outer ring on lower side (similar to Brook), yellow ring around black eye and yellowish bottom fins (opposed to Brook).

Cutthroat trout (Ct): Also called Native, only trout endemic to Wyoming. Yellow-orange-red color on lower jaw and gill cover, orange-red bottom fins (similar to Brook), small, black freckles on the back (opposed to Brook) and also over the yellow-green side. Hybridizes and crosses with rainbow and golden trout, producing many color variations.

Golden trout (Gdn): Originally found only in the headwaters of the Kern River in California, stocked in high altitude lakes in Wyoming. Brilliant red-orange gill cover and underbelly, yellowish side with about ten, black parr marks (chain of ovals) and with a carmine stripe along middle of side. Light-colored tip and black band on dorsal, pelvic and anal fins, pectoral and rest of pelvic and anal fins red-orange. Crosses often have much lighter coloring.

Mackinaw trout (Mcknw): Also called Lake Trout. A brook trout ("speckled") and lake trout ("lake") cross is called a splake. Mackinaw have wide color variations. Body generally blue-gray or bronze-green, with pale spots on sides and back, and on dorsal fin and tail.

Rainbow trout (Rbw): Blue-green back, sometimes spotted, blue-silver side grading toward white on belly. Faint pink band along side, pink bottom fins. For more information about wildlife and fish, write to the WYOMING GAME AND FISH DEPARTMENT, Communications Branch, Cheyenne, Wyoming 82002. Specific information about fish can be obtained from the following Drainage Area offices: For the Snake, Salt, Greys, Hoback, Gros Ventre and Buffalo Fork Rivers, tributaries, and lakes, write: Area Biologist, P.O. Box 67, Jackson, Wyoming 83001. For the Wind River, tributaries, and lakes (which includes the Washakie, Fitzpatrick and Popo Agie Wilderness), write: Area Fisheries Biologist, 260 Buena Vista, Lander, Wyoming 82520. And for the Green River, tributaries, and lakes (which includes the Bridger Wilderness and east slope of the Wyoming Range), write: Area Fisheries Biologist, P.O. Box 860, Pinedale, Wyoming 82941.

BACKCOUNTRY ETHICS

In an age when more and more of us are seeking the wilderness experience, turning to the high country for solace and solitude, it is vitally important that we observe certain precautions, lest we re-create the city squalor that we seek to leave. The great majority of backcountry trails in west-central Wyoming see little traffic, especially in early summer and fall. Indeed, it is easy to travel for weeks on end without meeting another person or seeing a tent or the print of a boot. However, the more popular trails, as identified in each specific text, suffer from crowded parking lots and constant hiker traffic. Dusty, rutted trails, fire rings at over-used camping sites, trees stripped of all dead wood, and other unappealing scars from human visitation all lessen the appeal of these once-pristine places. In well-used areas environmental damage increases each year and each person must share the responsibility in making the minimum physical and visual impact upon the land. The following list of backcountry ethics, if observed, will help assure that the pleasures of hiking and backpacking will be as great in the future as they are today.

PLAN YOUR TRIP. Study the many possibilities of where to go so you are not herded toward the over-publicized, over-developed tourist spots. If possible, schedule your trip for early summer or fall. Avoid the heavily over-used trailheads. And take time for a cross-country sidetrip to some destination that shows on the topo map but is bypassed by the trail. The rewards of solitude greatly outweigh the difficulties in finding it.

PACK IT OUT. The unspoiled beauty of a wilderness scene conveys a particularly refreshing feeling to its viewer. Few things mar this splendor more than litter: a trail map on the shore of an otherwise pristine lake, half-buried toilet paper under a tree clump, foil wrappers dumped behind a rock at a campsite. Although most veteran backpackers pride themselves in packing out all refuse, newcomers to the scene must be informed. Carry a litter bag on the outside of your pack for easy access and make a habit of collecting every scrap of paper, foil, fruit peels, bottles and cans for proper disposal outside the wilderness.

CAMP WITHOUT A TRACE. Even more of a problem than litter is the degradation of campsites. In areas of high use, trees have been stripped of branches, ground cover de-stroyed under boots and tents, and the natural beauty of sites replaced by sterile ground, ashes and half-burned logs. Fortunately, many backpackers who love the wilderness have changed their camping habits: No more camping next to the trail or near the river or along the lake shore; no more chopping, digging, lashing, and splicing woodcraft; no more campsite "improvement." The goal for nature-sensitive backpackers today is to camp so simply that later visitors to the site will find no trace of human use. Use gas stoves and foam pads instead of wood fires and bough beds. Leave the attractive dead branches on the trees and ground.

OBSERVE WILDERNESS SANITATION RULES. If you plan a trip with inexperienced city-people, make sure that they are "potty-trained" before they enter the wilderness. Toilet procedure is simple: Find a screened spot well away from travel routes, camping spots, and water. With the back of your heel kick a small hole through the ground cover to bare soil. After using, burn then bury the toilet paper, bury all waste and leave the area as you found it.

KNOW THE HAZARDS. Every hiker and backpacker who enters the backcountry takes with him the individual responsibility for his own comfort and safety. Know the symptoms and prevention of hypothermia and mountain sickness; learn how to camp in all kinds of weather conditions; become skilled with map and compass in case of disorienta-tion. . . .Educate others in the backcountry ethics and. . .

PLEASE LEAVE NOTHING BUT YOUR FOOTPRINTS.

FOR MORE INFORMATION

The names, addresses, and telephone numbers of the National Forest district offices in Wyoming relevant to this book are listed below. The number of the hiking trail is included under each appropriate office.

Kemmerer Ranger District
Bridger-Teton National Forest
P.O. Box 31
Kemmerer, Wyoming 83101
(307) 877-4415
 1   2   3

Gros Ventre Ranger District
Bridger-Teton National Forest
P.O. Box 1888
Jackson, Wyoming 83001
(307) 733-2752
 21   22   23   24

Greys River Ranger District
Bridger-Teton National Forest
P.O. Box 338
Afton, Wyoming 83110
(307) 886-3166
  4 5 6 7 8 9 13 14

Big Piney Ranger District
Bridger-Teton National Forest
P.O. Box 218
Big Piney, Wyoming 83113
(307) 276-3375
  10 11 12

Hoback Ranger District
Bridger-Teton National Forest
P.O. Box 1888
Jackson, Wyoming 83001
(307) 733-2752
  15 16 17 18 19 20

Wind River Ranger District
Shoshone National Forest
P.O. Box 186
Dubois, Wyoming 82513
(307) 455-2466
  25 26 27 28 29 30 31
  32 33 34

Pinedale Ranger District
Bridger-Teton National Forest
P.O. Box 220
Pinedale, Wyoming 82941
(307) 367-4326
  35 36 37 38 39 40 41 42
  43 44 45 46 47 48 49 50
  51 52

Lander Ranger District
Shoshone National Forest
P.O. Box FF
Lander, Wyoming 82520
(307) 332-5460
  53 54 55 56 57 58 59 60
  61 62 63 64

AUTHORS' NOTE

We spent a summer and fall in the Wyoming mountains, hiking the trails described in this guide and collecting the other necessary information. It was, without exaggeration, one of the most memorable and enjoyable experiences of our lives. Most paths took us deeper into the mountains to gather the facts firsthand, but others led us to people knowledgeable about each area, to the old-timers and the historians and the professionals. The opportunity to meet these exceptional people was a serendipitous pleasure, and without the benefit of their expertise and their encouragement, this book would not have been complete.

We especially would like to thank those who contributed directly to the selection of trails and who helped us with the historical data, and we refer the reader to them for further information. **In Kemmerer:** Rob Kominsky of the Kemmerer Ranger District. **In Afton:** Keith Wray of the Greys River Ranger District. **In Big Piney:** Rod Barker, R.O. Riley, and Al Murphy of the Big Piney Ranger District. **In Dubois:** Dale Hartman, Ted Knowles, and Gary Weigel of the Wind River Ranger District. **In Lander:** J.C. Whittekiend, Keith Parrish, Skip Shoutis, and Sid Freese of the Lander Ranger District. Also Chuck Viox, Fish Biologist for the Wyoming Game and Fish Department. **In Jackson:** Scott Phillips of the Hoback Ranger District and Ken Bronson of the Gros Ventre Ranger District. Also George Gruell, Wildlife Biologist and Ralph Hudelson, Fish Biologist for the Wyoming Game and Fish Department. **In Pinedale:** Don Stewart of the Pinedale Ranger District. And Glenn Dunning, Fish Biologist for the Wyoming Game and Fish Department.

In an effort to make future editions of this book up-to-date and useful, we invite any comment, correction, or suggestion. Please direct correspondence to the authors in care of Pruett Publishing Company, 3235 Prairie Ave., Boulder, Colorado 80301.
GOOD HIKING!

                                                               T.S.
                                                                S.S.

1

COMMISSARY RIDGE

One day trip or backpack
Distance: 6.8 miles/10.9 KM. one way
Hiking time: 5-5½ hours one way
Elevation gain: 3,310 feet/1,009 M.
Elevation loss: 1,430 feet/436 M.
Maximum elevation: 9,420 feet/2,871 M.
Season: Mid-June through September
Topographic maps:
  U.S.G.S. Fontenelle Basin, Wyo. 1967
  U.S.G.S. Pole Creek, Wyo. 1967
Kemmerer Ranger District
Bridger-Teton National Forest

The south end of the Bridger National Forest (west half) contains scenic, rolling ridges and plateaus, mixed cover of sage and spruce, pine and fir, and deep, interlaced drainageways. Unknown and unspoiled, little visited (except during hunting season), this region is a wildlife preserve, a wilderness with a small "w," currently unprotected by the National Wilderness Preservation System. Jeep roads, usually open from July through September, penetrate several of the valleys and follow the length of Commissary Ridge, but jeepers, as yet, are a very rare sight throughout most of the summer. Besides the Bluejay Creek Entrance to Commissary Ridge (described below), there are five other recommended starting points for hikers and backpackers: **Big Park Entrance,** north from Cokeville on the Smiths Fork/Big Park Road, for the Coantag Creek and White Saddle Trails and the Red Park Trail; **Spring Lake Creek Entrance,** on the Hobble Creek Road, for the Spring Lake Creek Trail to Lake Alice (see No. 2), the Hobble Creek Trail (see No. 3), and the Copper Mine Trail; **LaBarge Meadows Guard Station Entrance,** on the LaBarge Creek Road, for the Lander Cutoff Trail (No. 3) and the Hobble Creek Trail; **Little Corral Creek Entrance,** on the LaBarge Creek Road, for the Little Corral Creek Trail to Commissary Ridge, the Copper Mine Trail, the Poker Creek Trail to Lake Alice (No. 2), and the Coantag Creek Trail; **Pomeroy Basin Entrance,** on the Fontenelle Creek Road, for the Bear Trap Creek Trail and Roaring Fork Trail.

The unnamed trail from the Bluejay Creek Entrance enters the southeast end of the National Forest, and climbs up and over Absaroka Ridge, and climbs again to the top of Commissary Ridge. From here the double-tracked Commissary Ridge Trail, an excellent choice for a week-long trip, bears north through the 30-mile length of the range and gives access to exciting and truly wild places like Devils Hole Lakes, Electric Peak, Fontenelle Lakes, and Graham Peak. The trail connects with every other major trail in the range, providing for a variety of loop trips. Do not expect in this part of the Bridger National Forest the picnic tables and parking lots, the trailhead signs, carefully graded trails, . . . and the people, as found in the Bridger Wilderness. Go with topo maps (not available in Kemmerer) and a sense of adventure; be prepared for rough access roads and unsigned, unmaintained trails. The authors spotted antelope, mule deer, moose, elk and badger on their trip here. Rabbits, weasel, fox, coyote, porcupine, bear, etc, might also be seen.

Drive north from Kemmerer on U.S. 189 past the U.S. 30 junction and in another 0.7 mile come to the signed Wyo. 233 junction. Proceed on U.S. 189 for 4.7 more miles to an unsigned road, turn left and follow the main road across a stream, past cement foundations (right), and eventually under a power line. Cross a cattleguard at 11.7 miles from U.S. '189, loop over South Fork Fontenelle Creek at 23.3 miles, bend right at 24.8 miles where a sign reads "3 National Forest Boundary," and cross Clear Creek at 25.6 miles. Continue through a gate (please re-close) after 26.1 miles, then cross a cattleguard at the Bridger National Forest boundary, 27.8 miles from U.S. 189. Proceed another 0.6 mile to the Bluejay Creek crossing and park along the roadside beyond. Note: This rough, narrow access road often is passable only by pickups and four-wheel drive units from mid-June through mid-July.

From Bluejay Creek walk south back up the road to the first bend. Turn southwest onto a grassy jeep path (or turn at another jeep road farther southeast — see map) and soon curve right (west) on a climb to a sage knoll, 0.5 mile from the road. Here the view extends to forested hills of Absaroka Ridge southwest, to the sage rises and pasture lands around Fontenelle Basin south, and to rolling, sage hills in Oyster Ridge southeast. Sharp, white hogbacks of Mahogany Ridge can be seen also to the north. Drop west from the knoll into aspens and conifers, soon swinging left on a redblazed course. Proceed southwest past several game trail crossings, pick up a fence

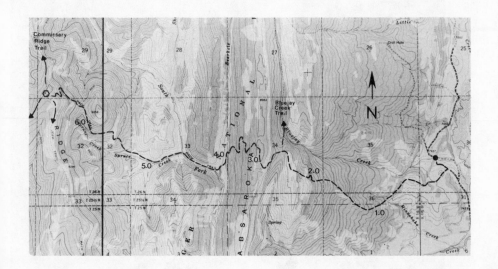

line to the left, then turn left through the open gate at 0.8 and cross the swampy headwaters of Minnehaha Creek. Follow blazes west-southwest through openings in the aspen where the trail narrows to a one-lane path and begin a steep climb into a coniferous forest.

Curve west, then northwest on the steady climb, gaining a good vantage of the Bluejay Creek drainage after 1.5 miles. Swing right (north) at mile 1.9 on a steep traverse up the first rise of Absaroka Ridge and loop north to a small bench near 2.6 miles — marked "8750" on the topo — above the north branch of Clear Creek. The Bluejay Creek Trail, a secluded, enticing alternate or loop route, forks north at this point and leads to the Indian Ridge Trail and the Bear Trap Creek Trail/Pomeroy Basin Entrance. To continue to Commissary Ridge, do not drop south into the Clear Creek Valley or north into the Bluejay Creek Valley but bear west then southwest on a final climb up Absaroka Ridge. Bend north at 2.8 miles, crest over the ridgetop after 3.1 miles, and drop on several steep, winding pitches into the Bearhole Creek Valley.

Wade the icy waters of Bearhole Creek at 4.2 miles, penetrate the steep-side South Fork Creek Valley on a west-northwesterly bearing, and come to the Spruce Creek confluence at mile 4.6. Cross South Fork Creek and stay along the right (north) side of Spruce Creek to the first large tree clumps at 5.2 miles, then swing northwest on a winding climb up the valleyside. Pass through a small saddle near 6.2 miles above the Spruce Creek headwaters and make a final, switchbacking climb to the top of Commissary Ridge, the 6.8 mile mark. Here jeep trails fork in three directions: south along Commissary Ridge, southwest and west into East Fork Creek Valley, and north along Commissary Ridge, the main access route.

Mule Deer

Salt River Range view

2 LAKE ALICE

Backpack
Distances:
   Commissary Ridge - 2.1 miles/3.4 KM.
   Lake Alice - 6.6 miles/10.6 KM.
Hiking time: 4-4½ hours one way
Elevation Gain: 890 feet/271 M.
Elevation Loss: 1.660 feet/506 M.
Maximum elevation: 9,420 feet/2,871 M.
Season: July through September
Advance topographic map:
   U.S.G.S. Wyoming Peak, Wyo. S.W. 734
Topographic map:
   U.S.G.S. Graham Peak, Wyo. 1967
Kemmerer Ranger District
Bridger-Teton National Forest

Over two miles long, filled with whopper cutthroat trout, lagoon-shaped Lake Alice makes one of the most attractive destinations for hikers in the south end of the Bridger National Forest. Two main routes provide access: an easy 1.7-mile trek from Hobble Creek Road up Spring Lake Creek to the more-visited south end, and a more adventurous climb up Little Corral Creek, then long drop along Poker Creek to the less-seen north end, as described below.

From the LaBarge Creek Road/Greys River Road/Smiths Fork Road tri-junction, drive south on the LaBarge Creek Road for 0.9 mile — crossing LaBarge and Little Corral Creeks — to the turnoff marked "Commissary Ridge 2/Alice Lake 7." Park alongside the road here or turn west and negotiate the rough jeep road for another 0.4 mile or so, proceeding across a sage flat toward the first tree clumps.

Begin hiking southwest up the jeep road and turn right onto an unsigned trail — marked by blazed posts near willow-filled Little Corral Creek — as the jeep road bends left (south). Soon enter a shady, spruce-and-fir forest on a gradual climb (where snow patches blanket the trail through mid-July). Drop right to a crossing of Little Corral Creek at 0.4 mile, pass branch tributaries on a climb above the creekbed, then drop left across the grassy valleyside to another crossing at mile 1.1. Now in view at the head of the valley is the 9,867-foot mountain, marked with a solitary post amid a small opening on the summit, where the Commissary Ridge Trail (No. 1) and the Copper Mine Trail connect. Cross and re-cross Little Corral Creek after 1.4 miles, bearing south-southeast into a valley more enclosed by conifers. Wind through fragrant spruce, fir, and pine on several more crossings, swing right (south) on a hillside traverse at mile 1.9, and climb steeply to the top of Commissary Ridge, the 2.1 mile mark and a worthy destination for a short, half-day hike. Here trail signs (sometimes fallen down) indicate directions east to the White Saddle Trail via Commissary Ridge, south to Alice Lake and Hobble Creek via Poker Creek, and west to the Copper Mine Trail.

Drop south from Commissary Ridge into the wide Poker Creek Basin, heading toward the rounded top and steep-sided cliffs of Mount Isabel on the skyline. Descend in and out of tree clumps for several hundred yards, swing right across Poker Creek at 2.4 miles and begin a steeper, switchbacking drop after 2.7 miles. Enter a grassy basin — a perfect campsite — at mile 2.8 where drainage-ways join from the left and right. Continue the gradual drop through grassy fields and avalanche paths, re-enter conifers and come to a red-blazed tree at 3.6 miles with a sign marking the turnoff to the White Saddle and Coantag Creek Trails, both excellent backpacking routes. Stay right for the trail to Lake Alice, soon passing a prominent drainage (left) which makes passage for the White Saddle Trail. Wind southwest to the valley bottom near mile 4.0, and descend past tributaries at 4.2 miles (right), 4.6 miles (left), and 4.9 miles (right). Then continue through sage past the 10,030-foot and 10,162-foot high points and connecting saddle of Mount Isabel (east), marked by a sign at mile 5.3.

Follow the rolling trail through conifer clumps and more sage, bearing toward the forested range which blocks the valley south. Pass an unmarked turnoff at 6.1 miles where a trail penetrates South Isabel Creek, then loops north toward Mount Isabel to connect with the White Saddle and Coantag Creek Trail. Curve carefully above the steep wash of Little Jo Creek at mile 6.3 and traverse a sage hillside for 200 more yards to a view of the Poker Creek arm of Lake Alice. Trails divide around the lake: one travels the west side around the Elbow Creek arm to Spring Lake Creek at the south end, another (sometimes obscured by deadfall) skirts the east side of Alice Creek, then climbs east and south to White Saddle.

Lake Alice inlet

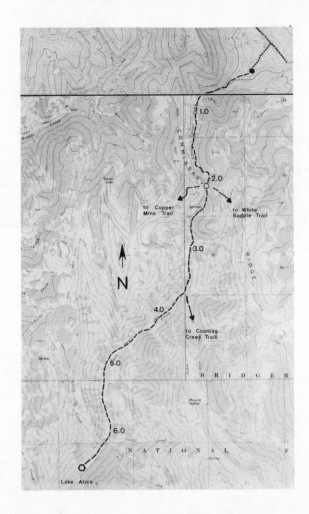

Creek crossing trick

3

LANDER CUTOFF TRAIL

One day trip or backpack
Distances: Gravesite - 2.6 miles/4.2 KM.
  "Hunters Knoll" - 4.3 miles/6.9 KM.
  Buckskin Knoll - 7.2 miles/11.6 KM.
Hiking time: 5 hours one way
Elevation gain: 1,600 feet/488 M.
Elevation loss: 2,590 feet/789 M.
Maximum elevation: 9,130 feet/2,783 M.
Season: July through September
Advance topographic maps:
  U.S.G.S. Wyoming Peak, Wyo. S.W. 734
  U.S.G.S. Afton, Wyo. S.E. 733
Topographic map:
  U.S.G.S. Porcupine Creek, Wyo. 1967
Kemmerer Ranger District
Bridger-Teton National Forest

In 1865 Congress authorized the construction of the Lander Cutoff of the Oregon Trail, the first Federally-sponsored road west of the Mississippi. General F.S. Lander paid Chief Washakie and the Shoshone tribe for a right-of-way through the Indian territory and then directed construction of the emmigrant trail from 1858 to 1860. The route left the original Oregon Trail near South Pass, made a difficult crossing through the Wyoming and Salt River Ranges, then turned north to Smoot (and eventually re-joined the Oregon Trail west of Fort Hall, Idaho. It saved 200 miles of travel through desert and larger valleys but was feared for its steep climbs and drops and rough course. Today the Lander Cutoff Trail is marked throughout its length by concrete posts and bronze emblems.

The trail from LaBarge Meadows Guard Station, also called the Buckskin Knoll Trail, retraces some of the historic route as it descends into Hobble Creek Valley and winds west to Buckskin Knoll. The wagon ruts have long since filled with grass here and only the splashing creek and rustling breeze now disturb the silence. But the spirit of the incredible transcontinental odyssey still seems to linger among the pines. During the hike visions of the scene of 100 years ago easily fill the imagination: Oxen bellow clouds of steam into the cool morning air, a dog barks at the scent of an elk, the dust-covered wagons rumble and creak over the rock here, tightly-locked, wood-spoked wheels slide down the muddy hollow there. And the pioneer father, with visions of a new life in Oregon, takes long, steady strides toward his destination.

Drive on the Smiths Fork Road — usually open by July — to the LaBarge Meadows Guard Station, 0.7 mile west of the LaBarge Creek Road/Greys River Road/Smiths Fork Road tri-junction. Follow the Guard Station road to the turnoff marked "Old Lander Trail/Commissary Ridge" and park nearby.

Hike northwest on a climb up the roadsize Lander Cutoff Trail, reaching a small saddle at 0.5 mile above a tributary of LaBarge Creek (left). Bend left (west-southwest), follow the concrete trail markers on another climb through conifer clumps, and break onto a ridgetop after 0.8 mile. The Commissary Ridge Trail forks south at this point and leads to the Copper Mine Trail in 3.3 miles and the Little Corral Creek/Poker Creek Trails in 3.6 miles. Stay right (west) on the double-tracked Lander Cutoff Trail, passing views of the steep-sided mountain south of Travis Lake at 166°/S. Bend left around the Hobble Creek headwaters, pass a hunter's campsite, then drop to a confluence of three tributaries at 1.6 miles which flow into Hobble Creek. Descend gradually through the scenic Hobble Creek Valley, crossing the creekbed several times, and come to the Estella A. Brown gravesite at mile 2.6 near an obvious, main tributary (right).

Turn right from the Hobble Creek Trail, a delightful alternate route which continues downstream for another 7.1 miles to the Hobble Creek Road, and climb gradually at 310°/NW to the left of the tributary. Climb steadily to a creek crossing at 3.4 miles, follow blazes on a bend left (west, then south) through towering spruce, then contour across a ridge after 3.8 miles and swing right (west) above a drainage left. End the gradual climb near a campsite at mile 4.3 on "Hunters Knoll," a possible turn-back point. To proceed to Buckskin Knoll, contour west onto the open flat and drop steeply north after 4.4 miles into the trees

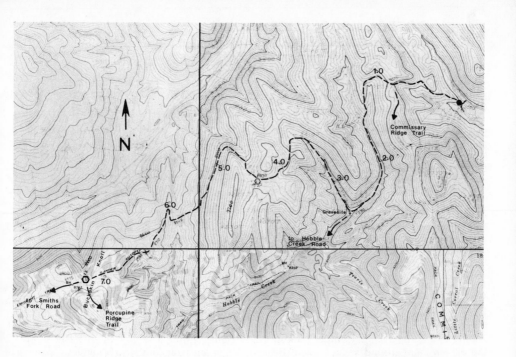

Emigrant grave

again. Make a long contour, curving left around a ridge at mile 4.8; drop southwest above the steep drainages of Smiths Fork (right) and loop around another ridge at 6.9 miles. Bend south again on a short ridgetop climb and eventually begin a final drop to the open plateau of Buckskin Knoll at 7.2 miles. From here the Lander Cutoff Trail drops another 2.2 miles to the Smiths Fork Road while the Porcupine Ridge Trail turns south and contours high above the west side of the Hobble Creek Valley.

4 COTTONWOOD, SLIDE, AND WAGNER LAKES

One day trip
Distances: Slide Lake - 1.7 miles/2.7 KM.
   Wagner Lake - 4.4 miles/7.1 KM.
Hiking time: 3-3½ hours one way
Elevation gain: 2,475 feet/754 M.
Elevation loss: 170 feet/52 M.
Maximum elevation: 9,785 feet/2,982 M.
Season: Early July through September
Advance topographic maps:
   U.S.G.S. Afton, Wyo. N.E. 740
   U.S.G.S. Afton, Wyo. S.E. 733
Greys River Ranger District
Bridger-Teton National Forest

Unlike the other hikes into the Salt River and Wyoming Ranges, the trip above Cottonwood Lake to Slide and Wagner Lakes departs from a setting more domestic than wild: Cottonwood Lake Campground. Camper-pickups fill the eleven campground spaces, local fisherman surround the lakeshore, angling for cutthroat and brook trout, and happy shrieks from children give audible testimony that they too enjoy this recreation area. In fact, for the three- and four- year-olds the campground makes an ideal base for the short hike to rugged, talus-lined Slide Lake. For the longer-legged hikers the pristine, wild amphitheater of Wagner Lake makes an appealing destination. However, snow melt does not dry from the alpine Wagner Lake Trail until mid- or late July. Another approach to Wagner Lake begins from the Smiths Forks Road below the Smiths Fork Guard Station and bears north and northeast along the wide Salt River Valley, reaching Wagner Lake after 11.8 miles. An excellent backpack trip, this trail sees little use and thus offers the alluring possibility of spotting deer, moose and other wildlife. Ct 10'', Brk 8'' in Cottonwood Lake, none in Slide and Wagner Lakes.

Drive on U.S. 89 south from Afton to the Cottonwood Lake turnoff, marked by signs. Turn east and proceed on the road — narrow and winding but easily passable by sedans — past the Cottonwood Lake Campground to parking at the west end of Cottonwood Lake, 6.5 miles from U.S. 89.

Follow the road along the northeast side of Cottonwood Lake for the first 0.4 mile. Stay left where a road turns right at 0.7 mile to the "Cottonwood Summer Home Area" and cross the auto bridge over Timber Creek in another 50 yards. Soon pass several campsites and wind through shady fir near Slide Creek (right). Enter a willow-filled basin after 1.2 miles and bear south to a bridgeless crossing of Slide Creek. Ahead rounded, scree mounds, snow-covered in July, frame the valley, and the connecting ridge forms a dam for Slide Lake, still unseen. After wading the creek, climb steeply on the single-lane trail, traverse through two switchbacks and break over the ridge at mile 1.5 to a view of the beautiful azure waters of Slide Lake, a nice lunch spot or turn-back point.

To continue to Wagner Lake, skirt the east side of Slide Lake with an easy climb and drop. Enter the Slide Creek Valley after mile 1.8, step the stones to the left side of Slide Creek in another 100 yards, and follow the valley on a curve right (south-southwest), passing another prominent drainage which leads southeast. Climb steadily to a view of spectacular cliffs on the skyline at 206°/SW, cross the creek and pass a rock-studded ravine (south) at 2.4 miles through which the trail will eventually pass, then swing north on a steep climb to a small bench near 2.7 miles. Traverse at 200°/SW up a sage hillside, contour south across a tributary at mile 3.0 and then southeast to the ravine at mile 3.3. After a steep climb up the ravine, reach a high saddle where the sheer, rocky Wagner Lake amphitheatre rises southwest and the deep Salt River Valley drops east. Turn right where another trail — an exciting route for a longer trip — bears left (east) into the valley, and make a final climb to the Wagner Lake bowl at 4.4 miles.

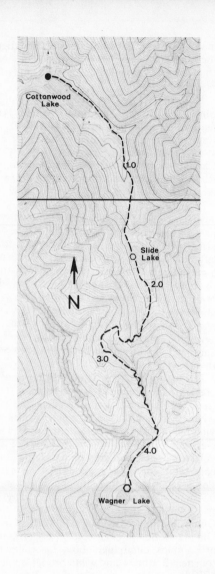

Cottonwood
Lake

1.0

Slide
Lake

2.0

N

3.0

4.0

Wagner Lake

Afternoon glide on Cottonwood Lake

5 PERIODIC SPRING AND SWIFT CREEK

Half-day trip
Distance: 0.8 mile/1.3 KM. one way
Hiking time: ¾ hour one way
Elevation gain: 480 feet/146 M.
Maximum elevation: 7,320 feet/2,231 M.
Season: Mid-June through October
Advance topographic map:
U.S.G.S. Afton, Wyo. N.E. 740
Greys River Ranger District
Bridger-Teton National Forest

Indians called it the "Spring That Breathes" and traveled great distances to bathe in the crystal waters and thereby cure their ills. In the 1890's an old-timber at the mill in Afton noticed its effect on the waters of Swift Creek — a puzzling rise and fall of water depth — and upon investigation discovered the cold water geyser that was the cause. Today called Periodic Spring, it is the largest of three fluctuating springs in the world and the only one in North America. Although scientists are unsure of the action that makes the water start and stop, one theory speculates that a natural syphon has been formed from an underwater lake. During the summer the spring flows freely but in early August, cycles begin to occur at about eighteen minute intervals. As figured for the information capsule, the hike to the Periodic Spring is only 0.8 mile, a fun and very scenic stop-off for bypassing hikers and for families with small children.

Another exceptional hike or backpack trip begins from the Swift Creek Trailhead and follows the valley east, then south-southeast to the top of the Salt River Range. This trip measures 6.8 miles one way to the 9,785-foot high point with an elevation gain of 3,345 feet and an elevation loss of 400 feet. The trail then connects with the Corral Creek Trail (No.8) on the east side of the range and — with arrangements for a pick-up at the Corral Creek Trailhead — makes one of the best trips in the Salt River Range. It compares favorably with any Wind River Range Trail with its rolling montane forest, sparkling streams, and rugged rock outcroppings, plus provides a better chance of seeing mule deer, moose, and other Wyoming wildlife.

Drive into Afton on U.S. 89/Washington Street and turn east onto Second Ave., marked by a sign reading "Swift Cr. Campground 2." Proceed onto a dirt road after five blocks, pass Swift Creek Campground, the power plant, and Balance Road, and continue to limited parking at the end of the road, 5.5 miles from U.S. 89.

Cross the footbridge over Swift Creek and head east-southeast into the scenic canyon, passing high rock bands, talus fields, and towering spruce. Cross a small footbridge to the left (north) side of Swift Creek at 0.4 mile, pass a magnificent stone outcropping which spans the valley like the broken wall of a dam, then re-cross Swift Creek on a bridge 200 yards above the last and come to an interpretive sign and a view of the Periodic Spring ravine. To get to the springhead, climb steeply south for another 150 yards or so between the massive ravine walls.

For the Swift Creek Trail, stay north of the creek at the trailhead **or** switchback north from the Periodic Spring Trail at the point when the dam-like outcropping comes into view, about 50 yards below the upper bridge (see map). Pass beautiful rock bands of gold, yellow, copper, and gray on a rolling contour east, and come to a good lookout of the Periodic Spring ravine and coursing water at 0.7 mile. Continue east along the valleyside, passing talus fields, scenic views of Swift Creek and fir trees decorated with wisps of Old Man's Beard. Loop left across a tributary at 1.5 miles, climb high above the valley bottom near 2.0 miles, and wind through conifers, hillside meadows and sage to the Rock Lake Trail junction at mile 2.5, sometimes unmarked.

Stay right on a slight drop where the Rock Lake Trail turns left and climbs, ford two branches of a tributary in several more yards, soon drop near Swift Creek and begin a curve right (south) through a wide basin. Cross beneath horizontal rock bands on the valleyside right after 4.0 miles, penetrate climax stands of spruce and pass a series of avalanche paths in the next two miles that sweep the mountainside above. After a winding climb along a ridge between two branches of Swift Creek, bear south-southeast toward the high, alpine saddle of Swift Creek Pass and reach the windy top at mile 6.8.

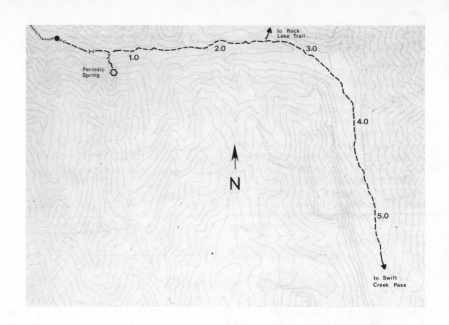

Periodic Spring chasm

6   LAKE BARSTOW

Half-day trip
Distance: 1.4 miles/2.3 KM. one way
Hiking time: 1 hour one way
Elevation gain: 420 feet/128 M.
Elevation loss: 40 feet/12 M.
Maximum elevation: 8,120 feet/2,475 M.
Season: Early July through September
Advance topographic maps:
   U.S.G.S. Blind Bull Creek, Wyo. SW 749
   U.S.G.S. Belford, Wyo. SE 748
Greys River Ranger District
Bridger-Teton National Forest

Unlike the many high ponds and tarns that dot the Salt River Range just under its crest, Lake Barstow is pocketed between two massive ridges well below the artic-alpine life zone. This location contributes to milder winter temperatures, a summertime habitat for insects and larvae, and thus, conditions that will support a trout population in the lake. And it's the chance of landing a large, ruby-gilled cutthroat that attracts the fishermen to Lake Barstow and makes this hike one of the most popular in the area. Another reason for its popularity is the short hiking distance. A rough timber road, passable by sedans in dry weather only, penetrates the North Three Forks Valley and reduces the trip to a short 1.4 miles, manageable even by junior fishermen. For a week-long backpack trip, combine this hike with one south to the Crow Creek Lakes (No. 7) or Corral Creek Lake (No. 8) via the Salt River Range Trail (see map). Be sure to pack a compass and obtain the essential U.S.G.S. advance proof topos (or the published U.S.G.S. topos when they become available in 1980) to aid in orienteering. FISH: Ct 10" in Lake Barstow.

From Alpine Junction drive south on U.S. 89/26 to the Greys River Road, marked with a mileage sign. Turn southeast, soon proceed onto the gravel road, and pass turnoffs to the Little Greys River Road at 8.7 miles, the Deadman Creek Road at 26.1 miles, and the McDougal Gap Road at 33.4 miles. Pass the Forest Park Campground after 36.0 miles and continue south another 3.4 miles to the North Three Forks Road, about 39.3 miles from U.S.

89/26. From the Tri-Basin Divide east of LaBarge Guard Station, drive north for 20.9 miles to the North Three Fords Road. Turn west onto the rough dirt road, cross a bridge over Greys River after 0.1 miles, then stay right where the South Three Forks Road loops left, and continue to an eventual crossing of North Three Forks Creek. Find parking in several more hundred yards where a left fork switchbacks and a right fork is washed out, about 3.1 miles from the Greys River Road.

Begin hiking at 280°/WNW up the old roadbed, heading toward a pointed, pyramid-shaped peak north of Lake Barstow. Bend left to a view of notched, 10,770-foot Rock Lake Peak at 248°/W which tops the Salt River Range, then bend left again toward an un-named, 10,490-foot peak at 216°/SW, marked with yellow-brown rock columns. Drop right across North Three Forks Creek at 0.3 mile, wind right then left toward the panorama of peaks, and soon cross a tributary. Come to a sign marking "Barstow Lake Trail" after 0.9 mile; turn right on a drop, then swing left through shady spruce and fir, cross a swamp and a tributary, and climb steeply into conifers. Continue the winding, uphill course to the left of North Three Forks Creek, contour along the narrow outlet and break out onto the east side of Lake Barstow at mile 1.4. An interesting log jam spreads across the mouth of the outlet here. Two avalance paths — white with snow through July — funnel down the steep south side of the lake bowl and inlet splashes noisily down the east side.

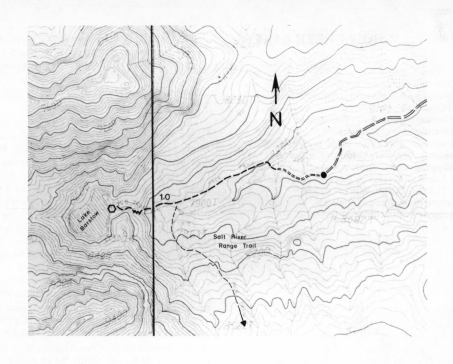

Lake Barstow fishermen

7 CROW CREEK LAKES

One day trip or backpack
Distance: 5.8 miles/9.3 KM. one way
Hiking time: 4½-5 hours one way
Elevation gain: 2,140 feet/652 M.
Elevation loss: 220 feet/67 M.
Maximum elevation: 9,320 feet/2,840 M.
Season: Mid-July through September
Advance topographic maps:
   U.S.G.S. Wyoming Peak, Wyo. N.W. 741
   U.S.G.S. Afton, Wyo. N.E. 740
Greys River Ranger District
Bridger-Teton National Forest

For the experienced backpacker the Crow Creek Lakes and Corral Creek Lake (No. 8) represent two of the most exciting and worthwhile destinations in the Salt River Range. Both trips to these lonely and wild places begin from trailheads along the Greys River Road and cross the Greys River — a raging torrent through July — on old "sheep bridges." The trails then climb west through deep, sage-and-conifer valleys and enter glacier-carved amphitheaters near the crest of the range. Beautiful wild-flowers such as western groundsel, skyrocket gilia, and shrubby cinquefoil color the hillsides along the trail, and the rolling Wyoming Range peaks form an impressive panorama east at the end of the hike.

Another excellent route to the Crow Creek Lakes, either for the trip in or for a loop return, follows the South Crow Creek Valley. Although the trail is not marked on either the Forest Service maps or the U.S.G.S. advance topo, the path shows plainly on the ground, as drafted onto the map photo. Near the end of the valley, the trail feeds into the Salt River Range Trail which then climbs north to the Crow Creek Lakes Trail. Notice the old sheepherder camps — littered with fire pits, old-style camp furniture, washbasins, and horseshoes — at the end of the South Crow Creek Valley.

Drive on the Greys River Road to the Sheep Bridge access across Greys River, 4.5 miles south of the North Three Forks Road junction (see No. 6) or 4.1 miles north of the Corral Creek Guard Station sign. Find out-of-the way parking along the roadside.

Hop over a couple of small brooks, cross the Greys River on Sheep Bridge at 0.1 mile, swing left (south) along a zig-zag pole fence and turn right through the gate at 0.2 miles into the Crow Creek Valley. Contour through grass and sage above Crow Creek (left) until coming to a large wash at mile 0.6, then either cross and re-cross the creek or traverse the steep, north hillside for 50 yards and re-join the trail just below a stand of dead timber. Pass a pool of water (left) at 1.0 mile, continue the rolling climb up the grass and sage valley, and cross two tributaries at 1.7 and 1.9 miles as the South Crow Creek Valley shows to the south-west. Enter clumps of lodgepole pine and deadfall, soon breaking to a vista of a steep rocky mountain wall at 244°/W which lies below unseen Crow Creek Lake. Maintain a gradual climb up the valley for two miles and turn right onto the Salt River Range Trail at mile 4.0 above an open basin at the valley's end. (The Salt River Range Trail also proceeds south, dropping and climbing past South Crow Creek and Little Corral Creek to Corral Creek (No. 8) in 3.7 miles.)

Climb steeply northwest and west — in July through beautiful, blue forget-me-nots — and swing west to a shady tributary near 4.2 miles Crest to the ridgetop at 4.7 miles after a switchback left, then fork left from the Salt River Range Trail (which bears north past Rock Creek, South Three Forks Creek to North Three Forks Creek below Lake Barstow (No. 6)) and make a steep, rocky ridgeline climb west. After a 200-foot elevation gain as the steep grade lessens, contour at 222°/WSW toward the steep-walled cirque which surrounds Crow Creek Lake. Swing south, then west over a protruding knoll after 5.6 miles and wind to the cirque basin at 5.8 miles. The lofty, 9,200-foot-plus lookout points on this final section bring into view a stunning array of rolling Wyoming Range summits east. Wyoming Peak (No. 9), highest in the range, shows at 125°/SE. To proceed to Upper Crow Creek Lake, cross to the far west side of Crow Creek Lake, contour up the rock-and-snow wall, and loop west above a Crow Creek tributary (south) into the higher cirque at 6.2 miles.

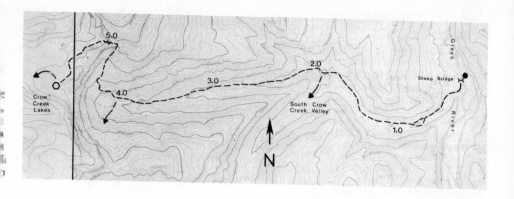

Trailhead fence

8
CORRAL CREEK LAKE

Backpack
Distance: 8.0 miles/12.9 KM. one way
Hiking time: 5½-6 hours one way
Elevation gain: 2,330 feet/710 M.
Elevation loss: 230 feet/70 M.
Maximum elevation: 9,540 feet/2,908 M.
Season: Mid-July through September
Advance topographic maps:
  U.S.G.S. Wyoming Peak, Wyo. N.W. 741
  U.S.G.S. Afton, Wyo. N.E. 740
Greys River Ranger District
Bridger-Teton National Forest

For the authors, the hike to the rocky, ice-carved amphitheater and snow-fed waters of Corral Creek Lake stands out as the high point of the several outstanding trips into the Salt River Range. The valley, wider and somewhat drier than nearby Crow Creek Valley (No. 7), is impressive with its steep, rock bluffs and, farther up, with its barren hillsides. Dainty, white long-leaf phlox, sky-blue forget-me-nots, and yellow western groundsel grace parts of the trail, and shimmering beaver ponds dot the valley bottom. Difficult creek crossings, a very close encounter with a mule deer, and a glimpse of camouflaged grouse added excitement to the authors' trip. But most memorable was the fleeting view of a brown bear as he loped across the trail and into a side tributary. FISH: Ct 10''-17''.

Drive on the Greys River Road to the "Old Sheep Bridge" across Greys River, 7.2 miles south of the North Three Forks Road junction (see No. 6) or 1.4 miles north of the Corral Creek Guard Station sign. Find out-of-the-way parking near the bridge.

Cross the stringers of the Old Sheep Bridge over Greys River, bend left (southwest) on a gradual climb up the embankment, and follow jeep tracks in and out of conifers, soon bearing at 130°/SSE toward the rounded mounds and rocky bluffs of Wyoming Range peaks. Pass through a climax stand of lodgepole pine after 0.2 mile, proceed by a crumbling log sheep pen (right), and come to signs marking the "Greys

River Stock Trail," etc. just before a view of Corral Creek. Swing right at 1.2 miles where the red Corral Creek Guard Station buildings show east across Greys River and continue on a near-level course into the Corral Creek Valley. Head at 238°/WSW toward a forested range south of Corral Creek; then bend right from the creek near mile 1.8, eventually enter scattered pine, and break to a viewpoint of steep, flat-topped bluffs at 274°/WNW. Follow the jeep road through rolling climbs and drops, cross a wash, and after 2.5 miles come to a view of another spectacular steep bluff south of the valley at 254°/W.

Cross a tributary at 3.0 miles and proceed along the wide valley floor as the view increases more and more to a wide panorama of steep bluffs ahead. Pass a tree clump (left) after mile 3.5 where sheep skeletons — victims of a sudden storm — litter the ground, and in 50 more yards skirt an old sheepherders camp (right). Enter more spruce and fir as the jeep tracks dwindle into one path, pass two large beaver ponds in Corral Creek (left) at 3.7 miles, then cross other tributaries at 4.2 and 4.6 miles and swing left on a crossing of the larger Corral Creek — fast and icy through July — at mile 5.2. (The Salt River Range Trail stays right above this crossing and proceeds on a northerly course to the Crow Creek Valley (No. 7) and beyond.)

Switchback west up a steep knoll where the vista soon encompasses the wide, pond-dotted valley east and the massive rock outcropping along the valleyside south. Begin a level walk along the knolltop after 5.4 miles, passing glimpses of Corral Creek north. Skirt the run-out of an avalanche path on the mountainside south at mile 5.7, cross a tributary and come to the second crossing of Corral Creek after 5.9 miles, an ideal destination — shaded, with continual water music — for lunch and turning back. To proceed to Corral Creek Lake, fork right near 6.1 miles where another trail branches left into a southerly valley and leads eventually to Cottonwood Lake (No. 4). Bend northwest after 6.4 miles, climb through switchbacks above a branch of Corral Creek (left), then dip across the creek at mile 6.9 and switchback southwest to the next ridge. Fork left at 216°/SW on a steeper uphill at 7.2 miles where the main trail continues north, and connects with the Swift Creek Trail (No. 5) on top of Swift Creek Pass, another 1.7 miles. Make a final climb northwest over the rocky, snow-washed trail and enter the steep-sided amphitheater of Corral Creek Lake at mile 8.0.

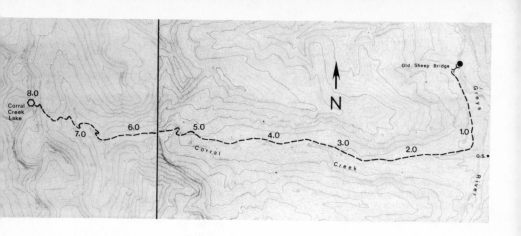

Corral Creek Valley

9   WYOMING PEAK

One day trip
Distance: 4.5 miles/7.2 KM. one way
Hiking time: 3-3½ hours one way
Elevation gain: 2,610 feet/796 M.
Maximum elevation: 11,380 feet/3,469 M.
Season: Early July through September
Advance topographic maps:
   U.S.G.S. Wyoming Peak, Wyo. S.W. 734
   U.S.G.S. Wyoming Peak, Wyo. S.E. 735
Greys River Ranger District
Bridger-Teton National Forest

That thrilling, I'm-on-the-top-of-the-world feeling is achieved with the ascent of Wyoming Peak, newly measured by the United States Geological Survey at 11,380 feet and highest in the Wyoming Range. A.D. Wilson of the historic Hayden Surveys made the first recorded ascent in 1877; later surveys have retained this lofty vantage as a triangulation station. Fire spotters were posted in the lookout shelter atop the peak until the early 1960's, and later a communications microwave tower was constructed on the summit, serviced via a new "high standard" trail. Although the microwave tower has recently been torn down, the trail to Wyoming Peak is in good shape, providing unobstructed access on a steady, 10% grade. Pick a good-weather day for this hike so you can stay on top of the summit and enjoy the vista. Pack binoculars for best viewing; wear gaitors through July for the snow drifts. Prepare for temperatures on the summit several degrees colder than the trailhead temperature and wind velocity three and four times as strong.

Drive on the Greys River Road to the signed junction with the Shale Creek Road, 8.9 miles south of the Corral Creek Guard Station sign or 3.6 miles north of the Tri-Basin Divide east of LaBarge Guard Station. Turn east, soon wind north then east again along Shale Creek to a "Y" at 2.3 miles, fork left (southeast) and loop north to the hilltop near the first band of trees, 2.8 miles from the Greys River Road. Park in an out-of-the-way spot along the roadside.

Turn right (east) from the road and pick a path through the lodgepole pine, staying near the north edge of a clear-cut slope. Swing left into the trees near the upper end of the clearcut, follow blazes through another bend left at 0.4 mile and cross an open hillside of sage and fir clumps. After passing an aspen grove, the trail leads to a panoramic lookout of the Salt River Range — from alpine peaks above the Crow Creek Valley at 294°/NW to the high north end of Commissary Ridge at 230°/WSW. Enter shady spruce — some with mammoth, four-foot diameter trunks — on a curve right and hook left at 0.5 mile across an open basin. Loop right then left through a steeper drainageway — a good water source — after 0.7 mile and bear at 310°/NNW through sage and blue silvery lupine. Then curve right into conifers at mile 0.9 and swing left through a drainage at 1.1 miles.

Climb steadily on a gradual curve right, now passing through twisted, gray-trunked limber pine as well as spruce and fir. Switchback right after 1.6 miles just before breaking out of the conifers, contour from southeast to southwest across the steep hillside; and switchback left (northwest) at mile 2.0 through more limber pine. Curve right again into thicker conifers on the northwest-facing hillside where snow cover holds through July, then switchback sharply right (southwest) at 2.4 miles in front of another north-facing snowpack. Contour south-southeast on a steady climb across the lofty, alpine hillside, winding through scree, exquisite tundra flowers, and wind-stunted fir. Switchback left (north-northeast) at mile 3.0 and continue the steady climb through red talus near 3.5 miles, bearing toward the tiny lookout shelter now in sight atop Wyoming Peak.

Switchback right at 4.2 miles to a post curve left toward the top of the peak, then make a final climb northeast through a series of short switchbacks and reach the rocky summit after mile 4.5. The square lookout shelter, weathered by snow and rain and battered by the constant winds at this high altitude, clings to the high point of the peak. It is locked and posted "No Trespassing." Near the north, east, and south sides of the lookout are stone triangulation markers from the 1933 U.S. Coast and Geodetic Survey. A vast and dazzling vista stretches in all directions: To the north and closest are the rolling, bare-dirt mounds of the Wyoming Range, colored with shale soils of red and yellow. Across the broad plains northeast and east-northeast, the sharp

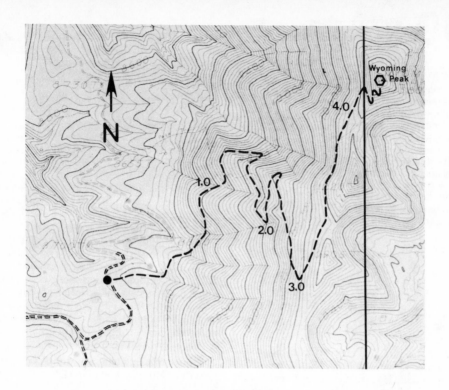

Wyoming Peak view

now-covered peaks of the Wind River Range rise into the skyline, with the highest including Gannett Peak at 35°/NE. And west beyond the verdant Greys River Valley, the massive summits of the Salt River Range loom skyward, most impressive in the afternoon sun when shadows reinforce the valleys and glacial amphitheaters in bold relief.

10 MIDDLE PINEY LAKE AND WOHELO FALLS

One day trip
Distance: (from east of Middle Piney Lake)
Upper Wohelo Falls — 2.6 miles/4.2 KM.
Hiking time: 2 hours one way
Elevation gain: 440 feet/134 M.
Elevation loss: 160 feet/49 M.
Maximum elevation: 9,160 feet/2,792 M.
Season: July through mid-October
Advance topographic map:
U.S.G.S. Wyoming Peak S.E. 735
Big Piney Ranger District
Bridger-Teton National Forest

The scenic Middle Piney Trail loops around the south side of MiddlePiney Lake and crosses the small, icy Middle Piney Creek to the north side of the valley. It then climbs gradually for another short mile to the white-water Wohelo Falls, a fun destination for an early, one-day hike. Beyond the falls at about mile 2.9, the Middle Piney Trail forks northwest and southwest: One trail switchbacks up the valleyside and continues to a junction with the Wyoming Range Trail east of Wyoming Peak (No. 9). The other stays in the valley, passes North Fork Fish Creek Trail, and picks up the Wyoming Range Trail farther south. The Wyoming Range Trail — highly recommended for a week-long backpack trip — traverses the length of the Wyoming Range through rugged and wild alpine country, linking Snider Basin south with Cottonwood Creek north (see No. 12). FISH: Rbw, McKnw in Mid. Piney Lk.

Drive on U.S. 189 into the middle of Big Piney, turn west onto Wyo. 350 and proceed 10.8 miles to a "Y" at the end of the paved road, marked by a mileage sign listing "20 Middle Piney Lake," etc. Fork right and continue past the Bridger National Forest boundary after another 10.3 miles. Stay right where a road to Snider Basin forks left at mile 10.5, angle left where the North Piney Creek Road forks right at 12.3 miles, then stay left again past the jeep road to the Straight Hollow Trail at 12.9 miles. Continue over the rough, narrow road, taking the right branch after 13.7 miles,

and come to camping and parking areas at the east end of Middle Piney Lake, 16.2 miles from the paved road and first "Y."

Pick up the trail south of the entrance road near the picnic area — a sign here reads "Middle Piney Trail," etc. — and begin hiking south-southeast through scattered spruce along the bottom of a small ravine. Soon climb out of the trees onto an open talus field where the view stretches across the shimmering lake waters and up the distant valley west. Especially eye-catching is a reddish, wedge-shaped mountain that forms the left side of the valley protruding into the horizon at 223°/WSW. Curve right through 40 more yards of talus, then follow the rolling trail into the cool shade of a spruce and fir forest. Cross two avalanche paths after 0.3 mile, now overgrown with 8-foot-tall seedlings. Hop a small tributary and continue on a half-mile contour through tall red-barked conifers. Through this section the lake (below right) sparkles through openings in the dark tree trunks, adding a bit of flamboyance to the otherwise serene scene.

Drop across an open gully and a small creek near the southwest end of the lake. Follow the level trail for 100 yards past a field of willow (right), then pass through a scattering of trees and wade two larger streams, ice-cold through July. From the second crossing in mid-valley a small, unnamed waterfall comes into view on the mountainside north, spilling white water into another tributary. To continue to the Wohelo Falls, stay about 20 yards above and right of the main creek and contour at 247°/WSW across a meadow where the trail is very faint. Look for a blaze after 60 yards and resume the easy, rolling climb back into conifers on a clear trail.

Break out of the trees to a small meadow after 2.1 miles, hop the rocks over another large creek which comes down the mountainside right, and after another 100 yards, look for the turnoff to the Lower Wohelo Falls marked with a sign. A well-blazed trail drops left from this point for 80 yards to the valley bottom and ends near the falls (actually a 40 foot stretch of snowy-white cascades). Violet sticky geranium, blue forget-me-not, and fragrant field mint line this access trail. Mist drifts through the air close to the cascades and the water makes a continuous roar — all in distinct contrast to the more tranquil forest floor above. Upper Wohelo Falls, a series of smaller, frothy cascades, lies upstream, reached with another 200 yards via the main trail.

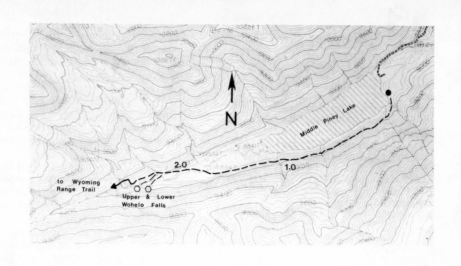

Lower Wohelo Falls

11 NORTH PINEY LAKE

One day trip or backpack
Distance: 4.7 miles/7.6 KM. one way
Hiking time: 3-3½ hours one way
Elevation gain: 1,575 feet/480 M.
Elevation loss: 1,240 feet/378 M.
Maximum elevation: 9,920 feet/3,024 M.
Season: Mid-July through September
Advance topographic map:
  U.S.G.S. Wyoming Peak, Wyo. N.E. 742
Big Piney Ranger District
Bridger-Teton National Forest

North Piney Lake, smaller by half than Middle Piney Lake and more secluded, makes one of the best destinations in the Wyoming Range for a two-day, or better, a three-day backpack/fishing trip. Two options exist for the access: A steep climb through Straight Hollow (sometimes called Long Hollow) to the top of the range, and then a ridgeline drop to the lake, as described below. Or an easier but less scenic, 5.3 mile trek up the North Piney Creek and Lake Creek Valleys (see map). To reach this latter starting point, turn right at the 12.3 mile mark onto the North Piney Creek Road where the Middle Piney Lake Road stays left. Drive past the signed "North Piney Creek Trail" after another 4.3 miles (an alternate but longer route) and park near an unmarked, westerly cutoff trail, 6.2 miles from the Middle Piney Lake Road. This trail, used by local fishermen, winds west to a small saddle at 0.6, drops south to the North Piney Creek Trail at 1.1 miles, and after 3.1 miles forks left (southwest) into the Lake Creek Valley. FISH: Ct, Brk.

Both the North Piney Creek Trail and the Lake Creek Trail feed west to the Wyoming Range Trail. Thus, loop trips can easily be arranged from North Piney Lake north to Menace Falls (No. 12) and Cottonwood Creek or south to Middle Piney Lake (No. 10) and farther south to Snider Basin. Be sure to take the essential U.S.G.S. topo maps.

From Big Piney drive west on Wyo. 350 for 10.8 miles to a "Y" at the end of the paved road, marked by a mileage sign listing "19 North Piney Creek," etc. Fork right, pass the

Bridger National Forest boundary after another 10.3 miles, and stay right past the road to Snider Basin at 10.5 miles. Bend left after 12.3 miles where the North Piney Creek Road forks right, then turn right onto a jeep road marked "Straight Hollow Trail" at 12.9 mile where the Middle Piney Lake Road proceeds left. Continue northwest to the trailhead parking area, 14.1 miles from the paved road and first "Y."

Pick up the unsigned Straight Hollow Trail down and left (southwest) of the parking area, enter a spruce and fir forest and bear northwest on a rolling climb to the right of the creek. Pass through a log fence, continue right of the creek for another 100 yards, then cross to the left side and pass a bubbling spring (left) — good spot for water fill-up — in 15 more yards. Climb steadily on a straight, 326°/NNW bearing for a half-mile, re-cross the creek at mile 1.3 where conifers block access on the left side, and continue the climb past a conspicuous avalanche run-out on the valleyside west. Soon pass clumps of tall, multi-trunked limber pine, cross to the left side of the creek — dry except in early summer at this point — and break into the open basin of Straight Hollow. Reenter conifers at the upper end of the basin and make a steep, switchbacking climb to the ridgetop at 2.3 miles. Here a beautiful view opens through the patches of limber pine, encompassing the unnamed, 10,700-foot-plus mountain range east of Middle Piney Lake at 160°/S.

Bear west, then southwest on a ridgetop climb along a wall of conifers right, gaining a high vantage of Straight Hollow below left. Contour into a slight saddle at mile 2.6, soon cross the ridge — the high point of the trip at 9,920 feet — and break out of trees to another panoramic vista. Rolling, brick-red peaks in the Wyoming Range —snow-capped through mid-July — rise to 10,800-foot elevations on the skyline at 245°/W, dotted with microwave antennas. The mountains continue to the right, dipping and rising like waves at 309°/NW near the end of the North Piney Creek Valley. Begin a steady drop down the north-facing hillside, cross a gulch at 2.7 miles, then curve right (northwest) and drop along a ridge. Pass glimpses of North Piney Lake west as the grade lessens, turn left on a hillside contour at 3.9 miles, then wind through tall lodgepole pine on a final drop to the lakeshore trail at mile 4.4, marked by a sign. Turn right (northeast) to get to the junction with the Lake Creek Trail.

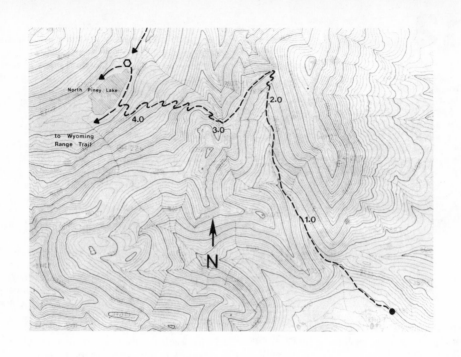

North Piney Lake

to Wyoming
Range Trail

4.0

3.0

2.0

1.0

N

Dusk at North Piney Lake

33

12 MENACE FALLS

One day trip or backpack
Distance: 2.9 miles/4.7 KM. one way
Hiking time: 2-2½ hours one way
Elevation gain: 1,090 feet/332 M.
Elevation loss: 140 feet/43 M.
Maximum elevation: 9,420 feet/2,871 M.
Season: July through September
Advance topographic maps:
 U.S.G.S. Blind Bull Creek, Wyo, S.E. 750
 U.S.G.S. Wyoming Peak, Wyo. N.E. 742
Big Piney Ranger District
Bridger-Teton National Forest

The hike to thundering Menace Falls via the North Piney Trail in the northern Wyoming Range contains aspects similar to many other Salt River and Wyoming Range trips, in distinct contrast to those in the Wind River Range. First, the drive to the trailhead follows miles of lonely gravel road and requires that careful attention be paid to the Bridger National Forest Recreation Map for orientation. Fellow travelers or ranchers from whom to ask information are few and far between. Second, the road peters out somewhere near the trailhead rather than end at a clearly designated parking area. Old logging road, jeep and horse trails, and gullies from creek run-off all look like possible courses. Third, the trailhead is unmarked and the trail itself is often less distinct than game trails. The Recreation Map is hopelessly inadequate in sorting out the different pathways, due to its lack of detail. Only U.S.G.S. topographic maps, with their larger scale and precise contour lines, provide the necessary information for orientation (see map photo). These topos, the first ever in the 7.5 minute series for this area, are scheduled for final publication in 1980.

Although the route-finding for the Menace Falls hike takes perseverance, the benefits of the splendid isolation more than compensate for the trouble. Here, again in contrast to Wind River Range trails, there are no hordes of hikers, no hillsides marred with the urban blight of flourescent tents, no meadows rutted with dusty paths. This area offers stunning scenery and a likely possibility of seeing wildlife. Unfortunately it currently remains unprotected by Wilderness legislation.

Drive to the South Cottonwood Creek Road in the Big Piney Ranger District by any of three access routes: 1) Turn east from the Greys River Road near Sheep Creek, cross McDougal Gap, and turn south to the South Cottonwood Creek Road about 1.3 miles after crossing North Cottonwood Creek. 2) From U.S. 189 turn west 1.6 miles south of Daniel onto the Ryegrass Junction Road, proceed west from Ryegrass Junction for about 9.6 miles, then fork south to the South Cottonwood Creek Road. 3) Head north on the Bare Creek Divide Road (F.S. 046) and intercept the South Cottonwood Creek Road 4.8 miles from Bare Creek Divide. From this last junction proceed southwest and west, passing Soda Lake after 2.1 miles. Cross Hidden Basin Creek and continue another 0.9 miles past ruins of a log cabin and corral (left) to a road "Y," marked with blazes. Find off-the-road parking nearby.

Stay left (southwest) on the blazed logging road where another road loops right (north) to a crossing of the South Fork just above South Cottonwood Creek. (This latter route leads to the South Cottonwood Creek Trail and also provides an alternate access to Menace Falls and to the Eagle Creek Trail, see map.) Contour through shady conifers for 0.5 mile, then swing right across the South Fork where the unmarked Eagle Creek Trail continues left to Eagle Creek. Come to a mileage sign near 0.7 mile reading "North Piney Trail/2 Menace Falls/4 Eagle Creek Trail/6 Roaring Fork Lake/11 Lake Creek Trail/14 Big Piney Road." Bear 239°/WSW over the double-tracked trail toward beautiful gray and red rock outcroppings on unnamed Wyoming Range mountains ahead, swing left (south) to a crossing of the South Fork at mile 1.9, and begin a gradual climb into the valley of the southerly tributary.

Contour south across a steeper hillside after 2.5 miles and come to the roaring white-water of Menace Falls at mile 2.7, above the confluence of westerly and southerly branches of the creek (see map)). The trail crosses the west branch of the creek and climbs south for several hundred more yards to a trail fork at 3.0 miles. Here the left trail stays in the main valley and soon reaches North Piney Pass and the North Piney Trail, while the right trail follows a small drainage on a 184°/SSW bearing to the Roaring Fork Lakes, another 2.7 miles.

Showy Fleabane

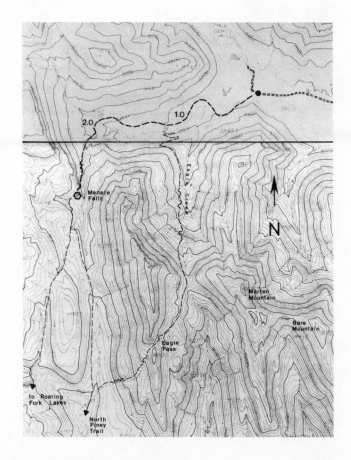

13 TELEPHONE PASS

One day trip or backpack
Distance: 8.1 miles/13.0 KM. one way
Hiking time: 5-5½ hours one way
Elevation gain: 1,370 feet/418 M.
Elevation loss: 1,405 feet/428 M.
Maximum elevation: 7,985 feet/2,434 M.
Season: July through mid-October
Topographic map:
  U.S.G.S. Pickle Pass, Wyo. 1965
Advance topographic map:
  U.S.G.S. Blind Bull Creek, Wyo. N.W. 759
Greys River Ranger District
Bridger-Teton National Forest

Don't look for a Mountain Bell booth on top of Telephone Pass. Only sage clumps and molehills cover this small saddle between the South Fork Greys River and Deadman Creek, and although it must have been crossed by an early telephone line, no evidence of pole or wires now remains. Few people venture up the valleys on either side of the pass: a rancher looking for strays perhaps, or an occasional wildlife photographer, or hunters during the big game season in October. But lacking the draw of a big fishing lake or any particularly outstanding vista, the area maintains its wilderness solitude. This backcountry loneliness, and the good chance to spot deer and moose, perhaps sandhill crane, are the main attractions of the trip. Use good judgement on the west crossing of the Little Greys River at the start; take topo maps or the map photo (right) for orientation and binoculars for wildlife viewing.

From Alpine Junction drive south on U.S. 89/26 to the Greys River Road, marked with a mileage sign. Turn southeast, proceed onto a gravel road after 0.9 mile, and continue to the well-marked junction with the Little Greys River Road, 8.7 miles from U.S. 89/26. Turn left (north), follow the gravel road past many signed creeks, and bend south onto a new road (not shown on Forest Service maps) near Bull Hollow. Pass McCain, Middle, and Stewart Creeks (right), then Broad Hollow (left, marked "Long Draw" on the U.S.G.S. topo), and come to the Telephone Pass Trail turnoff (right), 12.4 miles from the Greys River Road. Turn southeast, pass through a gate where an old silver sign reads "Stewart Trail No. 421," continue through the willow basin for 0.6

mile and park near another silver sig reading "Telephone Hollow Trail," etc. T get to the pick-up point, drive south on th Greys River Road to the Deadman Cree Road, another 17.5 miles from the Littl Greys River Road. Turn left (northeast) pass the Middle Ridge Trail at mile 0.4 an come to the Telephone Pass Trail after 1. miles.

Make a careful crossing of the Little Grey River, using safety ropes during the hig water of July. Climb gradually southwest o a jeep road to the top of a slight rise at 0. mile, then bend left into the spacious basi of Blind Trail Creek and bear toward th sharp, forested range of Deadman Mountai at 130°/SSE. Swing right across two sprin tributaries after 0.8 mile (the U.S.G.S. top shows one), pass a viewpoint of the Hobac Peak Range — a bare peaktop with a obvious cirque — at 74°/E near 0.9 mile, an continue through tree clumps with a ben right where another trail forks left to th Deadman Lookout Trail, as drafted onto th map. Cross Blind Trail Creek at mile 1.2 passing the corrals, benches and firepits o an old-style camp, and curve left on the jee road where the Hoback Peak Range agai shows at 74°/E. Keep the tributary of Blin Trail Creek on the left, bear 144°/SSE on th blazed trail where game trails cross, the cross a clearing at 1.7 miles and enter grassy field at mile 1.9.

Bend right to a 182°/SSW bearing throug silver sage, pick up the blazed trail at 2. miles upon re-entering trees, and drop into glen which opens to the right at 2.3 miles Fork left from the jeep tracks, bearin 167°/S; break into a second meadow – covered with sage — at mile 2.4 and hold southerly bearing through one of severa openings in the high willows around th South Fork Creek tributary. Cross th tributary at 2.6 miles, follow a clear tra through an extension of conifers shown o the topo, then enter the South Fork Valley a mile 2.7 and cross another tributary, no shown on the topo. Head for gray deadfall a the trail disappears into the sage and funne south into the obvious valley of South For Creek at 3.1 miles. Climb gradually to th left of the creek through tall pine and whit aspen, pass beneath boulder fields after 4. miles; soon cross and re-cross the creek an enter steeper, open hillsides at 4.8 miles filled with mountain bluebell and alpin

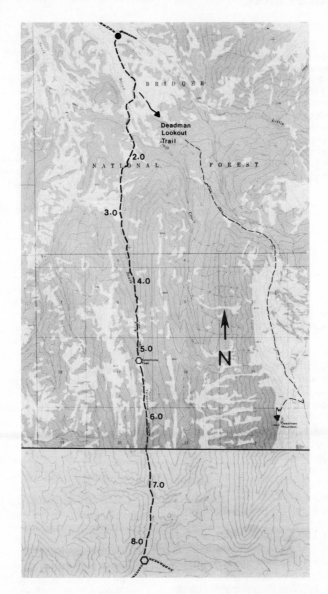

forget-me-nots.

Re-cross the small South Fork Creek at mile 4.9 as drafted onto the map; stay on the west side across several more tributaries and reach the open saddle of Telephone Pass at 5.1 miles. Here a beautiful vista of Wyoming Range peaks rises into view along the skyline south. To continue to the Deadman Creek Road, drop south into the steep Deadman Creek Valley; pass a drainage which opens left (east) at mile 5.6 and cross the left side of Deadman Creek at mile 5.9. Traverse through hillsides of larkspur, sticky geranium, western groundsel and forget-me-nots, cross and re-cross the creek after 6.8 miles and pass a viewpoint of the Deadman Mountain range at 52°/ENE through a tree-filled drainage at mile 7.3. Stay in the sage above the willows of the serpentine creek, now with a view of Salt River Range peaks at 206°/SW, and intercept the Deadman Creek Road at 8.1 miles.

14 BAILEY LAKE

One day trip or backpack
Distance: 4.7 miles/7.6 KM. one way
Hiking time: 3 hours one way
Elevation gain: 340 feet/104 M.
Elevation loss: 780 feet/238 M.
Maximum elevation: 7,300 feet/2,225M.
Season: July through mid-October
Topographic maps:
U.S.G.S. Pickle Pass, Wyo. 1965
U.S.G.S. Bailey Lake, Wyo. 1965
Greys River Ranger District
Bridger-Teton National Forest

Bailey Creek and Bailey Lake were named for the mountain man who hunted and trapped in this scenic valley west of Grayback Ridge at the far north end of the Wyoming Range. According to Mae Urbanek in *Wyoming Place Names*, Bailey built a cabin at the mouth of the creek and was first to pan gold there. Keith Wray of the Greys River Ranger District remembers another trapper's cabin near the lake (now gone) which dated probably to the 1800's. After the trapping era, the valley and surrounding mountains were explored mostly by sheep herders who, from the early 1900's to 1965, crossed the area via the sheep driveway. The hike, as described below, follows a downhill course after mile 1.5 through grassy meadows and stands of fragrant pine. Like the hike to Telephone Pass (No. 13), a main attraction is the possibility of spotting wildlife — deer, moose, water fowl — rather than any stunning panorama of peaks. FISH: Ct. 9''.

Drive on U.S. 89/26 to the junction with the Greys River Road south of Alpine Junction. Turn southeast, proceed onto a gravel road after 0.9 mile, and continue to the well-marked junction with the Little Greys River Road, 8.7 miles from U.S. 89/26. Turn left (north), follow the gravel road past many tributaries which are identified with signs, and bend south onto a new road (not shown on Forest Service maps) near Bull Hollow. Eventually fork right to "End of Road" where the left fork goes to "McCain Guard Station." Drive

another 0.4 mile to the trailhead, marked as "Bailey Creek Tr.," etc., 15.0 miles from the Greys River Road, and find off-the-road parking near a sign reading "Road Ends."

Pick up the faint trail left of the trail-head sign and head north-northwest through sagebrush for 200 yards. Soon follow a clearer trail near the bottom of a pine hillside (left) and a wide marsh (right), often the nesting area for pintail ducks. Begin a gradual climb into a small drainage after 0.7 mile, eventually swing northeast across the tiny stream, then bend north again near 1.0 mile and continue the easy climb through tall, gray-trunked pine. Behind, a beautiful panorama of mountaintops in the Wyoming Range, sparkling with snow through early July, shows above rolling banks of evergreens of the skyline. The high point is 10,361-foot Deadman Mountain at 147°/SSE, about 10 miles away.

Reach a slight saddle just before 1.5 miles — the high point of the hike at 7,300 feet — and begin a gradual drop through a small gully, staying right of the creek. After several hundred yards cross to the left side of the creek for a short distance, then recross and descend beneath open fields of grass (right) and hillsides of beautiful, pointed spruce and fir and long-trunked pine (left). Maintain the gradual drop along an open hillside, cross a small ridge after 2.6 miles, and soon loop through another main tributary, marked in blue on the topo. Pass the old "Stock Driveway" sign near 2.9 miles, stay high along the hillside as the valley deepens, then cross another tributary at 3.1 miles and continue north-northwest about 80 yards from the creekbed.

Proceed on a pleasant downhill traverse across rolling hillsides for another one-half mile until the deep green waters of Bailey Lake begin showing through the pine ahead. Stay right as the valley widens with beaver dams and grassy meadows, then loop right at 4.2 miles on a dry course around a tributary marsh — an area where killdeer can sometimes be seen — and soon come to the south end of Bailey Lake. The trail proceeds around the west side of the lake, drops through trees into another open drainageway, also filled with beaver dams, then loops right to a crossing over two tributaries and reaches the mid-point of the lake at 4.7 miles. At the north end of the lake the trail — clearly blazed and well-worn — enters tall lodgepole pine and descends northwest for 4.1 miles to the Snake River across from the Elbow Campground.

Raft on Bailey Lake

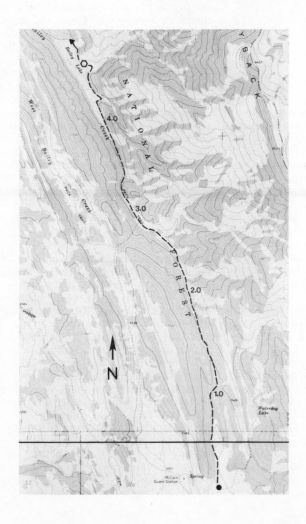

15 CLIFF CREEK FALLS

One day trip or backpack
Distance: 6.2 miles/10.0 KM. one way
Hiking time: 4 hours one way
Elevation gain: 1,100 feet/335 M.
Maximum elevation: 8,040 feet/2,451 M.
Season: Early June through mid-October
Topographic maps:
    U.S.G.S. Clause Peak, Wyo. 1965
    U.S.G.S. Hoback Peak, Wyo. 1965
Hoback Ranger District
Bridger-Teton National Forest

Little known except by locals around Bondurant, the Cliff Creek Trail penetrates a quiet, secluded valley south of Clause Peak and north of Hoback Peak at the northern end of the Wyoming Range. The terrain contains varied — and delightfully surprising — features: red bands of granite amid the surrounding, forested mountainsides after 1.3 miles, patches of wild strawberries — ripe during the first week in August — along the tributaries after mile 5.0, a sudden change from aspen and conifers to cottonwood trees at 5.1 miles, eroded and avalanche scrubbed hillsides beneath the runouts near 5.5 miles. But the scenic highlight of the trip is the fleecy-white, whispy Cliff Creek Falls at 6.2 miles, the most beautiful waterfall described in this guidebook. FISH: Ct 10'', in Cliff Creek below the trailhead.

From Hoback Junction drive east on U.S. 187/189 into the Hoback Canyon, pass the turnoff to the Granite Falls Recreation Area after 11.8 miles, and continue another 3.4 miles to the junction with Cliff Creek Road, marked with a sign. From Bondurant drive northwest on U.S. 187/189 for about 6 miles to the Cliff Creek Road junction. Turn southwest onto the dirt Cliff Creek Road and proceed 7.1 miles to the trailhead, marked by a mileage sign reading "Cliff Creek Trail," etc. Park along the roadside.

Wade (or drive) across the 15-foot-wide Cliff Creek — fast and icy through early July — immediately below the confluence of Sandy Marshall Creek, follow a jeep road south past a basin of willows for 0.5 mile, and look for a blazed, one-lane path which climbs right into conifers. Proceed on the path across a sage rise, drop through a tributary and continue in and out of trees over rolling terrain. Pass under a small talus field near 0.9 mile, stay right where a trail spur swings left toward the creek, and wind through towering pine to a sign marking "Snag Creek" at 1.4 miles. Continue up the valley beneath another sage hillside, now heading south-southwest toward a rocky, 10,140-foot extension of Hoback Peak.

Cross a small tributary at 1.6 miles, climb steadily on the wide, blazed trail into spruce and fir, then head south around a rise which blocks the view of Cliff Creek and cross two wide branches of Cabin Creek at 2.3 miles to a sign marking the "Ramshorn Trail." Climb to the top of a sage rise at 2.6 miles where signs indicate a turnoff east to "Bondurant Cr." and to the "Honeymoon Lake Trail," etc., then continue southwest up the rolling Cliff Creek Trail, passing through aspen and conifer groves and hillsides of brilliant, sunflower-like mules-ear wyethia which bloom from late June through mid-August. Veer next to Cliff Creek below red talus at 3.4 miles, drop left across the creek after 3.9 miles to a new trail (drafted onto the map), then contour through shady spruce and fir past the Hole-in-the-Wall Creek and re-cross Cliff Creek near 5.0 miles.

Pass several tributaries which wash an eroded, rocky hillside right, climb by an isolated grove of cottonwood trees — their gray, furrowed bark filled with gold lichen — and skirt above one mossy pond, then below another after 5.2 miles. Break into a meadow at 5.4 miles where two tributaries join, pass under the first of several avalanche paths after 5.7 miles, and contour up a more open, austere valley along the eroded cut of Cliff Creek. Near 6.0 miles come to the box end of the Cliff Creek Canyon where a small waterfall spills from the steep hillside west. The beautiful Cliff Creek Falls cascade down the tributary several hundred yards south, dropping first through a short upper fall, then falling freely for another 50 feet. On the hillside directly west a use trail, unmarked on the topo, leads south toward Cliff Creek Pass, Little Greys River, and Upper Hoback Canyon.

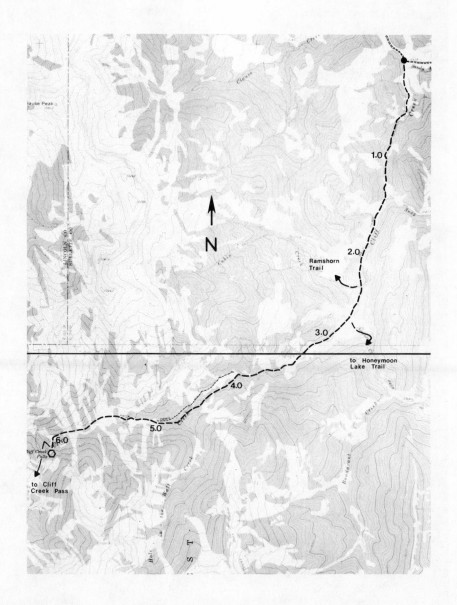

1.0

2.0

Ramshorn
Trail

3.0

Cliff

to Honeymoon
Lake Trail

4.0

5.0

6.0

to Cliff
Creek Pass

N

Cliff Creek Falls

16 SHOAL FALLS

One day trip or backpack
Distance: 5.6 miles/9.0 KM. one way
Hiking time: 4½-5½ hours one way
Elevation gain: 2,120 feet/646 M.
Elevation loss: 1,160 feet/354 M.
Maximum elevation: 8,540 feet/2,603 M.
Season: July through mid-September
Topographic maps:
  U.S.G.S. Granite Falls, Wyo. 1967
  U.S.G.S. Doubletop Peak, Wyo. 1967
Hoback Ranger District
Bridger-Teton National Forest

From a start just off Granite Creek Road, the Shoal Lake Trail climbs east into the Gross Ventre Range and reaches the Shoal Creek Valley with a view of spectacular Shoals Falls after 5.6 miles. This verdant valley bottom of beaver ponds and wildflowers, a destination for a strenuous one-day trip or, more easily, for an overnight camp, is claimed to be "one of the most beautiful areas in all of the Gros Ventre," according to oldtimer Dr. Donald MacLeod in an article in *The Living Wilderness* by Verne Huser. Further destinations include Shoal Lake, 3.1 miles above the Falls, Chateau Lake (where Grover "Slim" Basset caught the record eastern brook trout) via the Gros Ventre River Valley, and the Swift Creek Trail, a fast-dropping return route. FISH: Ct 9'' in Shoal Lake.

From Hoback Junction drive east on U.S. 187/189 for 11.8 miles to the junction with the Granite Creek Road, marked with a mileage sign reading "Granite Recreation Area," etc. Turn left (northeast) and continue on the main road for 8.0 miles to the Swift Creek Trailhead turnoff, 0.9 mile south of the Granite Creek Campground turnoff. Turn right onto the narrow, dirt road, cross the bridge over Granite Creek, then turn left where a sign reads "0.5 Swift Cr. — Shoal Lake Trail Junction," and find off-the-road parking in the next 0.4 mile.

Stay south of Swift Creek and follow the jeep road 100 yards east of the first trees to the motor closure sign. Begin a gradual climb onto the single path, cross a culvert over the Granite Ranch Ditch at 0.2 mile, and turn right (south) in 25 more yards onto the signed "Shoal Lake Trail." After a hillside traverse,

turn left at a signed junction near 0.4 mile and climb steeply, passing a good view of the sheer pinnacle called The Open Door on the skyline at 341°/N. Soon fork left where an unsigned use trail drops through aspen toward the Granite Ranch, climb steadily northeast into aspen then spruce and fir and come to lookouts of Ramshorn Peak behind at 218°/SW and a flat horizon of Gros Ventre mountains. Bear east across a small glen at mile 0.8, wind northeast to south through smaller openings, eventually traverse a hillside which slopes west to a Granite Creek tributary and break onto a ridge at 2.0 miles.

Swing right at 58°/ENE and climb gradually through the open grasslands, soon gaining a view of the treeless, rugged mountain northeast. Cross a willow-filled drainage at mile 2.2, traverse into an open meadow at 2.5 miles where the alpine mountain northeast again comes into view, then drop past a blaze through a small bowl and continue through flowered meadows to another high point at mile 2.7. Descend southeast and east after 3.0 miles, pick up the steep gully of West Shoal Creek (left), and after 3.4 miles drop east through switchbacks to a crossing of the creek. Stay right of a dry drainage (the U.S.G.S. topo shows an intermittent stream) and bear east through sage and conifer clumps for over a mile. Eventually swing right from the drainage to a hilltop view at 4.6 miles of 11,404-foot Palmer Peak at 30°/NE beyond the deep Shoal Creek Valley.

Drop and climb east through a grassy bowl and reach another viewpoint at 4.9 miles above Shoal Creek. Little Horse Peak can be spotted at 256°/W among other Gros Ventre Peaks on the skyline behind; slanted rock columns and steep mud flats comprise the unnamed, 10,493-foot mountain at 355°/NNE; and the flat top and glacial-cut face — banded with avalanche chutes — of Palmer Peak, now at 20°/NE, marks the north end of the range across Shoal Creek Valley. Drop northeast through a series of plateaus toward the valley bottom, loop left into a band of trees, then cross a small brook in willows and aspen and come to Shoal Creek at 5.6 miles, below several trout-filled beaver ponds. Any number of level, hard-ground spots at this point can serve as campsites, with a view of the three-tiered thundering Shoal Falls at 10°/N. To get to Shoal Falls and Shoal Lake, pick up the trail on the east valleyside.

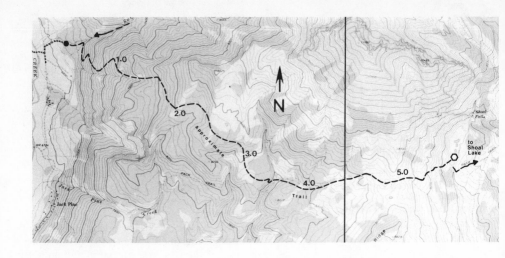

Beaver dam below Shoal Falls

Camp breakfast

17 GRANITE CREEK AND TURQUOISE LAKE

Backpack
Distance: 11.0 miles/17.7 KM. one way
Hiking time: 7-8 hours one way
Elevation gain: 2,480 feet/756 M.
Elevation loss: 80 feet/24 M.
Maximum elevation: 9,480 feet/2,890 M.
Season: July through mid-September
Topographic maps:
U.S.G.S. Granite Falls, Wyo. 1967
U.S.G.S. Crystal Peak, Wyo. 1967
U.S.G.S. Turquoise Lake, Wyo. 1965
Hoback Ranger District
Bridger-Teton National Forest

The dark green waters of Turquoise Lake fill a glacial-carved pocket high in the Gros Ventre Range — a setting similar to Blue Miner Lake (No. 23) — and make an exciting destination for a three or four day trip. Less distant destinations within the rugged, igneous rock walls of Upper Granite Creek Valley, determined only by your time and energy, beckon from every turn in the trail. A one-mile stroll takes you past steep granite walls and through fragrant fir and spruce groves; an eight-mile trek climbs to views of gray, snow-streaked Gros Ventre peaks. For longer trips over the Gros Ventre Range, see No. 18. Register overnight parking at the Hot Springs swimming pool office, open from 10:00 a.m. to 8:00 p.m. FISH: Ct 10''.

From Hoback Junction drive east on U.S. 187/189 for 11.8 miles to the Granite Creek Road junction, marked as "Granite Recreation Area," etc. Turn left (northeast), stay on the main road past turnoffs to Little Granite Road (1.5), Granite Ranch (7.0), High Line and Swift Creek Trailheads (8.0), and Granite Creek Campground (8.9), and park in the Hot Springs parking lot at the end of the road, 9.6 miles from U.S. 187/189. Additional parking, especially for overnight, can be found near the Granite Falls turnoff 0.3 mile back down the road.

Cross the Granite Creek footbridge and walk between the Hot Springs pool and red "changing" hut to the Granite Creek Trail, an obvious path unmarked by sign. Climb gradu-ally into shady spruce and fir beyond sight of Granite Creek, wind across a tributary and through small meadows with good views of sheer granite outcroppings left, and at 0.5 mile cross a rocky, 15-yard drainage. Skirt a marshy pond then a small hillside of boulders (left), eventually break into scattered conifers with a view of a blad, blunt peak at 3°/N, and follow the very rocky, winding path for over one-half mile east of a prominent ridge. Climb and drop through deadfall, then after 2.0 miles contour onto a hillside which rises steeply right toward the Gros Ventre Range.

Pass a sheer, granite wall which lines the west valleyside, and after 2.6 miles make a slight drop into a seedling-filled avalanche run-out. Proceed on a winding descent to a spacious meadow below another avalanche path at 2.8 miles. Loop near Granite Creek, wind through more gray talus then sage and avalanche debris, and after 3.6 miles pass the Bunker Creek drainage (west) on an easy climb up the wide valley. Climb steeply around a slight rise near 4.0 miles, pass through two bands of conifers, and at 4.5 miles skirt an open, rocky basin. Here the panorama encompasses the blunt peak seen earlier, now at 95°/ESE, and the long, sheer outcroppings and wavy talus fields of 11,107-foot Pyramid Peak at 345°/N, all blending to a gray landscape.

Pass a hunting camp across the creek at 5.1 miles, then follow the smooth, dirt trail through sage flats and tree clumps for several miles, arcing slowly northwest and west. With the gradual elevation gain, the view takes in more Gros Ventre peaks throughout the valley and, after 7.8 miles, extends for the first time to another spectacular range at 218°/SW, sharply glaciated and often pocketed with snow. Curve gradually left to a southwesterly bearing, climb steadily for two miles above the flat marshland in the valley bottom, and come to a trail fork in a tree clump at 9.8 miles, signed "Turquoise L. 2/2 Flat Cr. Div." In 25 more yards the most impressive vista of the trip appears on the skyline: the gray, scalloped 11,180-foot Gros Peak, often snow-covered through early August, tops the range at 203°/SSW, soon joined by the equally-rugged 10,594-foot summit at 218°/SW and 10,649-foot summit at 232°/WSW. Drop through a large tributary at 10.2 miles, the last before Turquoise Lake, continue climbing southwest on the clear trail, and after 10.9 miles make the final, short descent to the dark green lake waters.

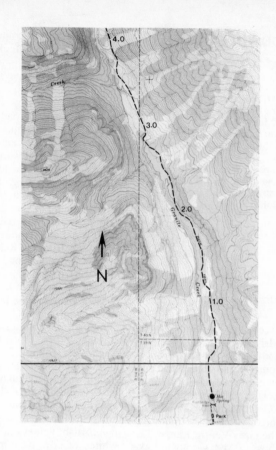

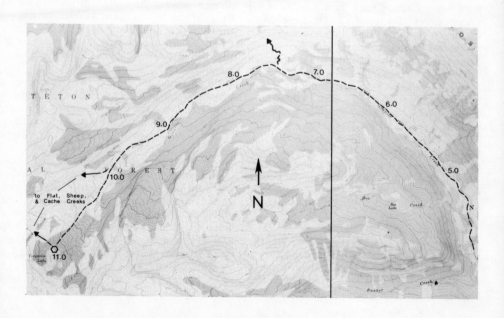

18 GOODWIN LAKE

Half-day trip
Distance: 1.7 miles/2.7 KM. one way
Hiking time: 1 hour one way
Elevation gain: 880 feet/268 M.
Maximum elevation: 9,500 feet/2,896 M.
Season: Mid-June through mid-September
Topographic maps:
U.S.G.S. Cache Creek, Wyo. 1965
U.S.G.S. Turquoise Lake, Wyo. 1965
Hoback Ranger District
Bridger-Teton National Forest

Picture-postcard scenes of the Teton Range highlight both the drive to the trailhead and the short hike to Goodwin Lake. But given its proximity to the tourist-jammed Grand Teton National Park, this trail remains surprisingly uncrowded, especially in September. For backpackers, Goodwin Lake makes an ideal first-day destination on a three or four day trip into the heart of the Gros Ventre Range. Extended trip variations: 1. From Goodwin Lake south past Jackson Peak for 3.9 miles to a "four-trail junction" west of Cache Peak, then west down Cache Creek for 8.4 miles to the Cache Creek Trailhead. 2. Or west down Cache Creek to the Game Creek turnoff, then southwest into Game Creek (see No. 19). 3. From the "junction" west down Cache Creek for 3.0 miles to the Granite-Highline Trail turnoff, then southwest on this beautiful alpine trail — newly re-marked — for 14.0 miles to Granite Creek Valley. 4. From the "junction" east for 2.4 miles to Turquoise Lake (see No. 17). 5. From the "junction" north into the seldom-seen Flat Creek Valley for 9.1 miles to the Flat Creek Trailhead. Note: The adjacent National Elk Refuge permits vehicular access to the National Forest via Curtis Canyon and Flat Creek Roads only. FISH: Goodwin Lake, Brk 9".

Goodwin Lake memorializes an early mountain man of Jackson Hole whose favorite trapping areas were at the heads of the Sheep, Flat, and Nowlin Creeks. Goodwin trapped the area in winter long before any white men had settled there the year around. Each fall he

brought in a pack train of supplies and traps and then sent his stock back home to Idaho since he lacked winter feed for them. In spring he cached his furs and walked to Idaho for his pack train.

Drive on U.S. 187, 89, & 26 into Jackson. Proceed east on Broadway past the National Elk Refuge Headquarters, soon turn left through the Refuge entrance gate, and follow the main road toward the Curtis Canyon Campground, coming to the campground turn-off after 7.5 miles. Stay left here, drive through several switchbacks, then stay right after 9.2 miles at the Sheep Creek Road junction and continue over rough road to the Goodwin Lake Trailhead parking, a total of 11.7 miles from the Refuge gate. If snow melt or rain has made bad road conditions, find off-the-road parking before the last two switchbacks near mile 10.7.

Turn left from the road where a sign reads "Goodwin L. Tr./Goodwin L. 2" and begin climbing east-southeast up a one-lane trail, staying near the left side of an old clear cut of slash and seedlings. Soon enter scattered pine and after 0.2 mile continue past rolling meadows, covered in mid-summer with a variety of wildflowers — blues and violets of silvery lupine, wild blue flax, sticky geranium, and purple aster, reds of scarlet gilia and paintbrush, yellows of western groundsel and whites of cow parsnip. Follow the obvious path up a short, steep climb, pass a trail that joins from the left after 0.4 mile, and proceed along a ridgetop through shady limber pine for the next one-half mile. Occasional openings in the trees here give glimpses east across Sheep Creek Valley to a sheer rock wall which forms the rugged, lower reaches of the 10,263-foot summit.

Climb gradually around the left side of a knoll near 0.9 mile, then break out of the trees on a level traverse to a tributary creek, unmarked on the topo. A large path of boulders, conspicuously bare of vegetation, cuts above and below this drainage, creating an unusual and interesting terrain feature. Cross these boulders, continue south on the rock-studded path and soon pick up Goodwin Lake Creek on the left. Step stones to the left side of the creekbed after 1.5 miles and break to a view of Goodwin Lake in 20 more yards. Paths loop around both sides of the lake: the right (west) fork recrosses the creek and passes beneath a steep hillside of talus while the left fork circles through trees to a campsite in several hundred more yards.

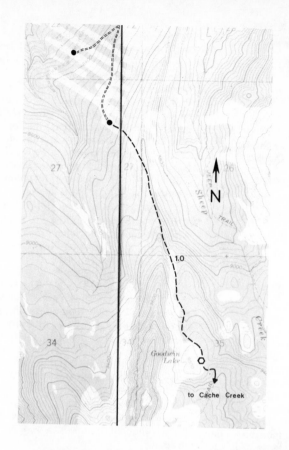

Tent dweller at Goodwin Lake

19 CACHE CREEK AND GAME CREEK

One day trip
Distance: 5.2 miles/8.4 KM. one way
Hiking time: 3-3½ hours one way
Elevation gain: 730 feet/223 M.
Elevation loss: 770 feet/235 M.
Maximum elevation: 7,410 feet/2,259 M.
Season: Mid-May through mid-October
Topographic map:
   U.S.G.S. Cache Creek, Wyo. 1965
Hoback Ranger District
Bridger-Teton National Forest

An easy, scenic hike just outside of Jackson, the double-tracked Cache Creek Trail penetrates southeast through the Cache Creek Valley into the Gros Ventre Range. It is popular with day hikers, backpackers, and dudes on commercially-guided horsepack trips. In the fall of 1976 the Forest Service improved the Cache Creek Road access, established a new trailhead and motor closure near Salt Lick Draw, and imposed a regulation prohibiting camping for about the first mile of trail. The trip, as described below, stays in the Cache Creek Valley to the Game Creek turnoff at mile 2.8, then climbs the range to a saddle — a nice turn-back point — and drops into the Game Creek Valley. For other trips of three and four days, see Goodwin Lake (No. 18).

Drive on U.S. 187, 89, & 26 into Jackson. Proceed east on Broadway to Redmond Street (nearly opposite the St. John's Hospital entrance), turn right (south) and drive five blocks to Snow King Avenue. Turn left, continue straight ahead as Snow King Avenue becomes Cache Creek Road, and come to the new trailhead parking area at the end of the road, about 2.2 miles from the Redmond Street turnoff. Arrange for a pick-up on the Game Creek Road, a turnoff from U.S. 187 6.3 miles south of the Wyo. 22 junction.

Begin hiking over the jeep road along the left side of Cache Creek. Bend left (southeast) for 30 yards across the tributary in Salt Lick Draw, then swing right and continue the very easy climb up the valley, passing stands of delicate aspen on the hillside left and pools of still water near the creekbed. After 0.6 mile stay left where a trail drops right to an established campsite with log benches, tables, and fireplace, reserved for Special Use Permittees. Eventually separate from the creek on a westerly bearing and pass open hillsides of grass and wildflowers near Gin Pole Draw at mile 1.4. Here a wide basin slopes toward the creekbed, giving view to a beaver lodge and beaver dams, and to pole frames of two tent cabins farther beyond in the conifers.

Enter the sudden shade of conifers after 1.8 miles as the mountainside and creekbed close in from both sides. Follow the roadbed on a long, gradual curve right, cross a main tributary after 2.5 miles that flows from the Gros Ventre Range north-northeast, and in several hundred more yards come to a trail turnoff, marked "To Game Creek." The rocky north top of Cache Peak shows at 81°/E beyond the Cache Creek Valley from this point, balanced on the left and right by two other rugged Gros Ventre peaks. Fork right onto the Game Creek Trail, wade 20 feet of water to cross Cache Creek — ice-cold and fast through July — then follow a double path upstream for 15 yards only and turn sharply right onto a hillside traverse. The double path, more conspicuous than the shaded traverse, continues upstream for another 100 yards into a steep tributary drainage.

Climb steadily west-southwest above the Cache Creek Valley and eventually curve left along the west side of a basin to a level saddle at 3.4 miles. Here exquisite wildflowers— geranium and paintbrush and lupine—dot the hillside, while ever-rustling aspen line the drainage south. A thickly-forested cone at 130°/SSE creates a scenic backdrop, all making this secluded saddle a worthwhile destination, perhaps the turnback point. To proceed to Game Creek, drop south through a grassy basin, climb to a knolltop at 3.8 miles, then drop more steeply down one drainage and pick up another drainage which joins behind left at 4.0 miles. Although the trail on the topo forks south toward the ridge at mile 4.1, stay in the drainage (marked with an intermittent stream but showing no evidence of water until a spring just above the meeting with Game Creek) and continue west. Pass a series of beaver ponds—haven for pan-sized Brook trout — which fill the main branch of Game Creek (right) and end the hike at a pick-up car on Game Creek Road, a total distance of 5.2 miles.

Cache Creek

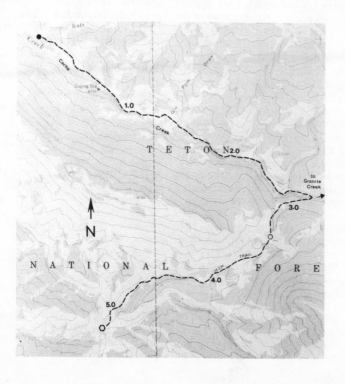

20 SKI LAKE

Half-day trip
Distance: 1.5 miles/2.4 KM. one way
Hiking time: 1 hour one way
Elevation gain: 760 feet/232 M.
Maximum elevation: 8,720 feet/2,658 M.
Season: Early June through mid-October
Topographic map:
   U.S.G.S. Rendezvous Peak, Wyo. 1968
Hoback Ranger District
Bridger-Teton National Forest

The cool waters of Ski Lake lie within a talus-and-grass cirque in the southern reaches of the Teton Range. The hiking distance is short, the trail well-worn and popular, traveled by strings of dudes on horseback from a dude ranch and by backpackers headed toward the towering Teton Range peaks, as well as by day hikers. For a longer trip, a use trail, drafted onto the map, leads to Phillips Pass and connects with the Phillips Canyon Trail, Teton Crest Trail, and Mesquite/Moose Creeks and Coal Creek Trails. By mid-July beautiful wildflowers of reds, yellows, and violets color this area: sticky geranium, silvery lupine, scarlet gilia, western groundsel, and wild blue flax. FISH: Ct 10''.

Drive southwest and west out of Jackson to the Wyo. 22 turnoff. Proceed across the Snake River and through the small Wilson hamlet, soon cross the bridge over Fish Creek, then continue for another 4.3 miles to the Phillips Canyon Road, marked with a sign. Turn right (north) onto the rough dirt road, drive another 0.7 mile and find an off-the-road parking spot anywhere in the next 0.2 mile. If road conditions are bad—a definite possibility in early summer or after rainstorms—stop after only 0.4 mile near a small jeep road which forks left. The blazed trail branches left in another 100 yards as this jeep road drops back to the Phillips Canyon Road.

From the parking area farther down the road, begin hiking northwest on a cross-country climb straight up the sage slope and intercept the obvious trail after about 60 yards. Turn right (north), follow the trail left then right through a prominent gully, then swing left (north) again and continue in and out of conifers for 200 yards to the edge of a meadow. At this 0.5 mile mark the trail — unsigned — divides: double tracks cross the meadow north, leading to a junction in another 1.8 miles with the Phillips Canyon Trail, and a single path bends left toward Ski Lake. In view here is 10,927-foot Rendezvous Peak with its bare alpine side, on a 354°/NNE bearing over 3½ miles away, framed on the left by the closer, round 9,582-foot knob.

Follow the Ski Lake Trail across the tiny Phillips Canyon Creek just beyond the fork and eventually wind west-northwest back into scattered tree clumps, staying above a tributary (right). Cross the tributary near 0.9 mile, stay to the right of it for 25 yards, then veer right across a sage-covered basin, heading toward a grove of aspen and conifers. Bend left again as willows in the Ski Lake Creek basin come into sight farther north, make a short, steep climb past an old campsite (left), and continue the steady climb west-northwest. Soon this elevation gain yields a beautiful panorama of distant, sky-blue mountains: due south the Snake River Range breaks into the horizon, southeast rolling, hazy peaks mark the northern Wyoming Range over 30 miles away, and east-southeast the Gros Ventre Range begins, more rugged than the others and often covered with vivid snow patches through early August.

End the steady climb with the added view of the wide Snake River Valley southeast and a better vantage of the surrounding mountain ranges. Re-enter tree clumps, swing right across Ski Lake Creek after 1.4 miles, and in another 20 yards come to the deep-green waters of Ski Lake. The dainty lake bowl is girded by thick conifers on the south side, a rocky, 9,584-foot knob spills a fan of talus into the water on the far west side, and farther right a run-off creek splashes noisily down the steep bank. To extend the hike, follow the unsigned use trail on a steady climb up the ridge north of Ski Lake. Proceed west to the divide top, reaching the 9,734-foot summit near the 3.0 mile mark. Drop along the divide to a ridgetop cut-off west to Coal and Mesquite Creeks at 3.5 miles, or stay on top of the divide around the Middle Fork amphitheater, drop slowly and curve east to Phillips Pass at 4.8 miles.

Sunlit leaves

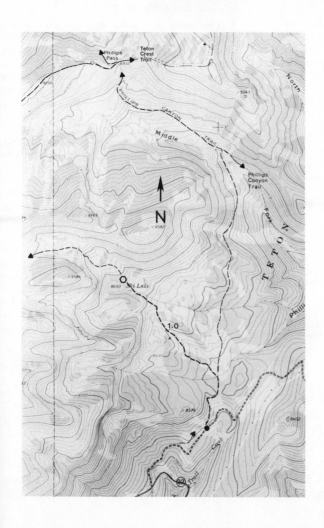

GROS VENTRE SLIDE GEOLOGICAL AREA

Half-day trip
Distance: 0.8 mile/1.3 KM. one way
Hiking time: 1-1½ hours one way
Elevation gain: 720 feet/219 M.
Maximum elevation: 7,640 feet/2,329 M.
Season: Mid-May through mid-October
Topographic maps:
 U.S.G.S. Shadow Mountain, Wyo. 1968
 U.S.G.S. Blue Miner Lake, Wyo. 1968
Gros Ventre Ranger District
Bridger-Teton National Forest

"Gigantic Landslide Dams Gros Ventre River Three Miles above Kelly Tuesday" headlined Jackson's Hole Courier of June 25, 1925, telling of one of the largest recent earth movements in the world. After exceptionally heavy rainstorms, the north end of Sheep Mountain — some 50 million cubic yards of sandstone of the Tensleep formation — had broken loose from underlying shales and roared into the Gros Ventre River over 2,000 feet below. The resulting 225-foot dam formed a body of water, known today as Lower Slide Lake, which inundated ranch lands and several buildings. Although believed to be permanent by the state engineer and state surveyor, the upper 60 feet of the dam gave way on May 18, 1927. The devastating flood, described as "a terrific unexplainable roar of grinding and hissing and swishing water," swept through the town of Kelly 3½ miles downstream, destroying most of the buildings and killing six people.

Today a raw scar about 1 mile long and 2,000 feet wide marks the Gros Ventre Slide site, a scene featured often in Geology textbooks. Boulders can still be seen 300 feet up the slope of the Red Cliffs opposite the slide where they were tossed by the massive wave of earth. Of the original buildings in Kelly, only the church with its beautiful stained glass windows remains, now serving as the post office. A 0.4 mile interpretive trail loop has been built by the National YWCA and the U.S. Forest Service next to the Gros Ventre Road and provides an excellent introduction to the Gros Ventre Slide and Kelly Flood. But to really appreciate the enormity of the occurrence, you must hike into the area itself, a difficult cross-country trek through thick vegetation,

loose fields of talus, and mounded and pocketed ground cover.

The authors discovered that the least difficult access is via the main drainageway, as figured for the information capsule and described below. Only high, earth banks along the east fracture line mark the slide near the start but after a steady increase in elevation, large boulder fields and irregular earth mounds in the path can be seen. Also in view soon are the beautiful, rolling Red Hills on the eastern horizon and the distant, familiar spires of the Teton Range at 301°/WNW. From the vantage point at 0.8 mile, a good appreciation is gained for the immensity of the slide. A vast sea of angular boulders — some displaying rose and yellow and gray colors, others decorated with black lichen or gold crystal — sweep upward some 2,000 feet higher toward the top of Sheep Mountain.

The route along the drainage can be extended to the top fracture line with an estimated 1½-2 more miles of slow, difficult climbing, an adventurous all-day trip for the experienced rock climber. Or, as shown on the map photo, a loop can be made west to ponds in the middle of the slide path. The small, upper pond, trapped in a pocket of large boulders, appears fairly deep but shows no inlet or outlet. The larger, lower pond, also stagnant, is bordered by conifers and aspen and contains schools of salamanders. Other ponds, unmarked on the topo, lie farther down the hillside north. For the easiest return, cross the mesa east and drop back down the drainage. **Wear good, thick-soled hiking boots; be careful of falling or sliding rocks!**

Drive on U.S. 187, 89, & 26 to Gros Ventre Junction. 0.5 mile north of the bridge over the Gros Ventre River and marked with a sign listing "Gros Ventre Road/Campground/Kelly," etc. Turn northeast onto the Gros Ventre Road, pass the campground turnoff at 4.8 miles and Kelly at 7.2 miles, and turn right where the Antelope Flats Road branches left at 8.4 mile. Continue another 4.7 miles to the Glenn Taylor Ranch turnoff, 150 yards west of the Gros Ventre Slide Interpretive Trail pullout. Turn right onto a narrow dirt road, cross the bridge below Lower Slide Lake after 0.5 mile, and after 80 more yards, turn right onto a jeep road. Park in the next 100 yards along roadside.

Hike southwest along the jeep road, staying right of the creek marked on the topo. Swing left toward the drainageway where the road

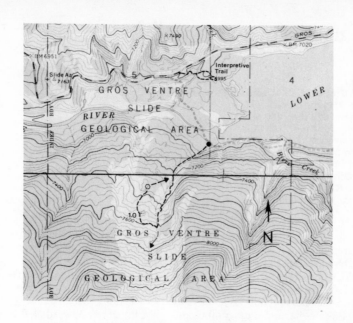

Gros Ventre slide rubble

bends right, follow the creekbed through shady conifers for 300 yards, then climb the hillside left and find an easier course above brush near the drainage and below the steep slide wall (left). Proceed on a slow climb through loose rock, keeping away from the steeper slide wall. After 0.4 mile climb past a flat, grassy mesa 200 yards right, continue the climb to a view beyond aspens of the pond on the mesa, then pick a winding course through large boulders and eventually climb past a large island of conifers (left) at 0.8 mile.

22 GRIZZLY LAKE

One day trip
Distance: 3.6 miles/5.8 KM. one way
Hiking time: 2½ hours one way
Elevation gain: 820 feet/250 M.
Elevation loss: 654 feet/199 M.
Maximum elevation: 7,620 feet/2,323 M.
Season: Mid-May through mid-October
Topographic map:
  U.S.G.S. Grizzly Lake, Wyo. 1965
Gros Ventre Ranger District
Bridger-Teton National Forest

In early summer when deep snowdrifts still hide the high mountain trails and only glacier lilies are in bloom along the wet hillsides, the lower and drier trail to Grizzly Lake makes the best choice for a day's hike. In midsummer the open trail becomes hot and dusty and the marshy Grizzly Lake — haven for dragonflies and frogs — takes on a stagnant appearance, a marked contrast to the crystal-cool waters of Blue Miner Lake, for example. But by late fall when snow again has covered the high country, this trail, lined with tawny, rustling grasses and tangy sage, offers excellent hiking. Pick up drinking water in the many tributaries of East or West Miner Creeks for the rest of the trip. And be sure to take time to explore the elaborate series of beaver dams which cross the tributary near 1.7 miles. FISH: None, possibly to be re-stocked.

Drive on U.S. 187, 89, & 26 to Gros Ventre Junction, 0.5 mile north of the bridge over the Gros Ventre River. Turn northeast onto the Gros Ventre Road, proceed past the campground turnoff at 4.8 miles and the Kelly townsite at 7.2 miles, and turn right after 8.4 miles where the Antelope Flats Road branches left. Stay on the Gros Ventre Road around Lower Slide Lake, pass the Red Hills Campground and the Crystal Creek Campground, and continue another 0.1 mile to off-the-road parking, 12.5 miles from the Antelope Flats Road.

Intersect a grassy jeep road, signed as "Miners Creek Trail," which begins south of the Gros Ventre Road, 15 yards west of a sign reading "Approaching Forest Camp." Follow the road south then west on a gradual climb for 80 yards, fork left onto a single path near the knolltop, and contour southwest through sage and tree clumps for several hundred yards, heading toward the upper end of a buck fence. The view through this section encompasses sheer, blue-gray cliffs of the Lavender Hill north and sculptured, brick-red bluffs of the Red Hills north-northwest, and then extend to the jagged spires of the Teton Range on the far horizon northwest, impressive even from this 22 mile distance.

Stay about 20 yards left of the buck fence pass through a stand of pine near 0.6 mile, and climb a small rise where the Red Hills show again on the skyline north-northwest. Drop and climb steeply through the East Miner Creek drainage at mile 0.9, then again through the West Miner Creek drainage at mile 1.2 Curve right where a trail forks left up another creek (misnamed on an old sign as "West Miner Creek") and after 1.5 miles cross the creekbed to a sign reading "3 Grizzly Lake/1 Sheep Mtn." Climb steeply southwest along the right side of the drainage, cross to the left side as the creek veers sharply northwest, and follow the blazes for several more yards to the Grizzly Lake/Blue Miner Lake trail fork at 1. miles, marked by a sign.

Fork right, then follow blazes around a new beaver pond (right) where several yards of the old trail are now under water. Swing right to a muddy creek crossing 200 yards above the pond, wind west through sage for 25 yards toward a conspicuous dead pine, then pick up a clearer trail and climb steadily to a knolltop at 2.3 miles. Begin dropping west toward a clump of conifers and soon bend right toward the distant Teton Range. Eventually pass a grassy bog, drop through a wash and curve north at 2.8 miles into a wide valley, marked on the topo with a stream but showing little evidence of water. Follow the hillside contour on a bend left, then proceed on a level, pleasant course through fields of grass and high sage for one-half mile and drop through scattered pine to the blue-green waters of Grizzly Lake at 3.6 miles.

Aspens at West Miner Creek

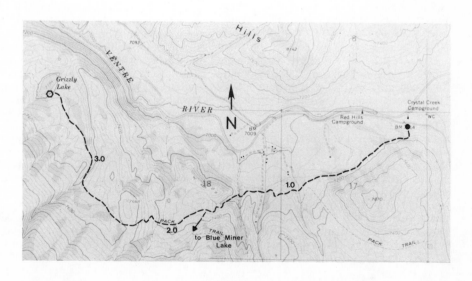

23 BLUE MINER LAKE

Backpack
Distance: 6.6 miles/10.6 KM. one way
Hiking time: 5-5½ hours one way
Elevation gain: 2,970 feet/905 M.
Elevation loss: 590 feet/180 M.
Maximum elevation: 9,770 feet/2,978 M.
Season: July through September
Topographic maps:
   U.S.G.S. Grizzly Lake, Wyo. 1968
   U.S.G.S. Blue Miner Lake, Wyo. 1968
Gros Ventre Ranger District
Bridger-Teton National Forest

Of the many lakes within the Gros Ventre Range, none surpasses pristine Blue Miner Lake for its rugged setting and wild beauty. Jagged boulders, covered with black lichen, dam up the lake waters near timberline, and snow and talus on Sheep Mountain provide an awesome backdrop. But the price of admission to this wilderness spectacle is steep, quite literally: the arduous climb figures at almost 3,000 feet elevation gain and takes the better part of a day. Plan on two, or even better, three days for the trip to have leisure time to explore the area. Camping spots, sheltered from the usual wind, can be found 50 yards down from the lake below the rocks. FISH: None.

Drive on U.S. 187, 89, & 26 to Gros Ventre Junction, turn northeast onto the Gros Ventre Road and proceed to the Blue Miner Lake Trail parking area, following the driving instructions in Grizzly Lake (No. 22).

First, hike from the trailhead to the Grizzly Lake/Blue Miner Lake trail fork at 1.7 miles, as described in the third and fourth paragraphs of Grizzly Lake (No. 22). Stay left where the trail to Grizzly Lake turns right toward a beaver pond. Follow a slight ridge on a 180°/SSW bearing, soon contour onto a hillside of sage and wind on a steady climb for about 200 yards, watching for a blazed pine higher on the hillside left. Switchback left on a 52°/ENE bearing on a climb beneath the blazed tree, follow blazes with a curve right where the path is grassy and obscure, and after 2.0 miles proceed east on a level contour through scattered tree clumps and grass-filled openings. Behind, the view looks down onto the beaver pond near the trail fork and also includes the high bluffs of the Red Hills north-northwest and the pinnacles of the Teton Range on the far horizon northwest.

Swing right to a gradual climb along a prominent ridge after 2.2 miles where the view overlooks the deep West Miner Creek and Crystal Creek Valleys. Climb steadily southwest on a clear trail to the right of the ridgetop, penetrate thick fir and spruce for several hundred yards (another trail stays on the ridgetop), then turn left at a blazed arrow and make a steep climb of 100 yards to the top of the ridge. Pass an opening with a conspicuous dead tree in another 30 yards, unmarked on the topo, and continue up the ridge to another opening near 3.3 miles, marked on the topo with the elevation "8,497." Here a steep dropoff of red rock — a good destination for a one day hike — gives view to a high escarpment at 204°/SW near a summit of Sheep Mountain.

Drop slightly through a saddle for 200 yards, then make a long, steep climb along the ridge and after 4.1 miles veer left to the edge of another steep dropoff. Here the vista extends for 46 miles to sawtooth peaks in the Wind River Range at 100°/ESE, noticeably more rugged than the surrounding, and much closer, Gros Ventre Range. Swing right (west) from the overlook through a clearing — filled with silvery lupine, sky-rocket gilia, western groundsel, wild blue flax, and other beautiful wildflowers in July — and climb south through spruce and fir, then gray-trunked, twisted limber pine until breaking into a high, alpine meadow at 4.5 miles. Stay near the middle of the meadow when the trail fades among grass and flowers and make a mile-long traverse southwest as the rock-and-snow wall of Sheep Mountain rises into view ahead, then becomes hidden again. Watch for a blazed limber pine along treeline left of the meadow at 5.5 miles, follow blazes for 200 yards across another basin, and continue past the final tree clumps to the steep edge of the Blue Miner amphitheater at 6.0 miles. Beautiful banded rock, talus fields, and chiseled cirques from the tarnished copper-green waters of Blue Miner Lake at 210°/SW and another unnamed lake at 150°/SSE. Continue west along the edge to a cairn which marks the access down to Blue Miner Lake, as drafted onto the map photo.

Blue Miner Lake amphitheater

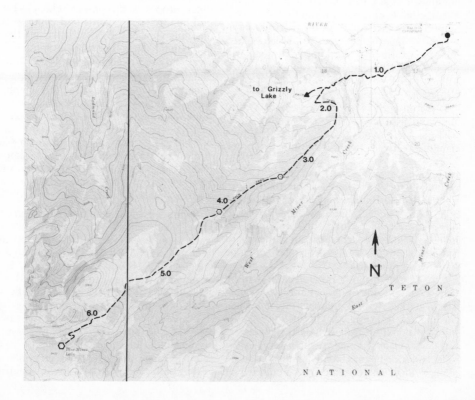

24 THE SIX LAKES

Backpack
Distance: 11.2 miles/18.0 KM. one way
Hiking time: 7-8 hours one way
Elevation gain: 3,020 feet/920 M.
Elevation loss: 1,220 feet/372 M.
Maximum elevation: 9,540 feet/2,908 M.
Season: Late June through mid-October
Topographic maps:
   U.S.G.S. Upper Slide Lake, Wyo. 1965
   U.S.G.S. Darwin Peak, Wyo. 1967
Gros Ventre Ranger District
Bridger-Teton National Forest

Distant views of the jagged Wind River and Teton Ranges, a closer, looming panorama of Gros Ventre Peaks, brilliant July wildflowers, dry sage hillsides and cool stands of conifers all are passed on the long hike to The Six Lakes. Serene and shimmering, the cluster of lakes (count 'em: five, or seven or eight) lies beneath a majestic, L-shaped range with Crystal Peak north through unnamed, 11,000-foot summits to Black Peak south, a most inviting destination. Pack water for the first 7.1 miles; allow at least three days for the trip; take camera rather than fishing gear to the lakes. See map for shorter destinations; very long trip possible to Chateau, Brewster and Lunch Lakes. FISH: Six Lakes, none; Jagg Creek, Ct, small.

Drive on U.S. 187, 89 & 26 to Gros Ventre Junction, proceed on the Gros Ventre Road past the Kelly townsite at 7.2 miles, and turn right (east) after 8.4 miles where the Antelope Flats Road branches left. Stay on this road past both Lower and Upper Slide Lakes, eventually fork left where another road angles right to Goose Ranch, and drive another 0.4 mile to the signed "Goosewing Guard Station" turnoff. Turn right and continue 0.2 miles to trailhead parking in front of the Guard Station, about 21.5 miles from the Antelope Flats Road junction.

Cross through the horse corral behind the Guard Station and intersect the Goosewing Trail, marked with a sign of trail mileages. Switchback up a hillside of rustling aspens, follow the obvious trail on a bend right across tiny Yellowjacket Creek (usually dry) at 0.7 mile, and soon begin a steady climb southwest along a ridge. The winding Gros Ventre River

Follow an exceptionally scenic route south along the ridge after 4.1 miles which overlooks the deep Crystal Creek Valley west and takes in more rolling hills of the Teton Range on the horizon. After 4.5 miles begin a one-half mile ramble southeast across the top and down the side of an open knoll. Re-join the trailcut at a post at mile 5.0, soon cut across marshy Two Echo Park (Try the echo!), and continue the southerly bearing beneath the cool canopy of lodgepole pine. After a long, switchbacking drop break into a spacious park near Jagg Creek at 7.1 miles, the first dependable "watering hole" since the trailhead and often the campsite of dude outfits. Continue through the park to the left of Jagg Creek, cross a tributary at 7.5 miles and eventually bend southeast, take a left fork and climb steadily through conifers to the top of a rise. Here the gray Gros Ventre cliffs, topped with rocky columns that look like battlements of a medieval castle, appear on the skyline at 177°/SSW.

Break out of trees onto rolling, sage hills at 8.6 miles; pass through a barbed wire fence at 9.4 miles and immediately fork right as the left fork continues to an eventual drop into the Bear Cabin Creek drainage. Climb south through sage then conifers to the hilltop at 9.8 miles, drop west through switchbacks for several hundred more yards and come to an enchanting view of the "first" lake and the rock cliff behind. The other lakes lie southwest and west and are linked by several use trails.

and distant sage and conifer bluffs show occasionally west-southwest on this climb, and from the ridgetop at 1.4 miles, the view looks down a long, sage hillside to the forested basin of Tepee Creek. A small pond catches the eye at 110°/SE, and on the horizon south-southwest steep, unnamed peaks, slate-gray and streaked with snow through early August, mark the Gros Ventre Range south of The Six Lakes, almost 11 miles away.

Swing west and maintain elevation across the "8890" hillside for one-half mile, then climb southwest to another ridgetop at 2.4 miles where the vista expands again to distant ranges. 13,804-foot Gannett Peak, highest point in Wyoming, can be discerned on the hazy skyline at 108°/SE, surrounded by white Mammoth and Minor Glaciers. Other jagged Wind River Peaks show to the right of that bearing, a distance of over 44 miles away. And to the south, the sheer, gray cliffs of the Gros Ventre Range can again be seen. Follow the rolling path southwest by a marshy pond at 2.8

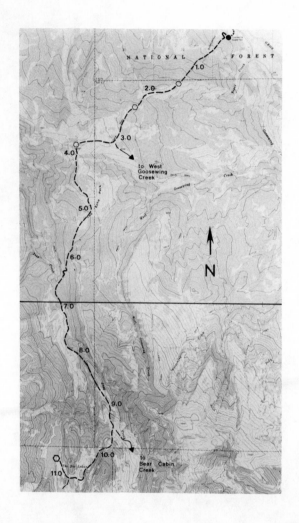

miles and pass an unsigned ridgetop trail after 3.1 miles which drops to West Goosewing Creek. Curve gradually left around a spacious sage basin which holds a northern branch of West Goosewing Creek and come to a sign reading "White Canyon" near tree clumps at

mile 3.9. From the ridgetop a few yards beyond, the veiw stretches some 28 miles to a skyline of spectacular Teton Range spires. Highest is the famous, 13,770-foot Grand Teton at 285°/WNW; also prominent is the bulky, square-topped Mt. Moran at 300°/NW.

Lake reflections

Beaver

25 UPPER BROOKS LAKE

One day trip or backpack
Distance: 3.3 miles/5.3 KM. one way
Hiking time: 2-2½ hours one way
Elevation gain: 175 feet/53 M.
Elevation loss: 135 feet/41 M.
Maximum elevation: 9,160 feet/2,792 M.
Season: Early July through September
Topographic map:
  U.S.G.S. Togwotee Pass, Wyo. 1965
Wind River Ranger District
Shoshone National Forest

Soaring, two-mile-long breccia cliffs rise west of Brooks and Upper Brooks Lakes and create a scenic impact at the trailhead which rivals the vista of Squaretop Mountain seen from the Green River Lakes (No's. 36 & 37). And the Pinnacle Buttes and other unnamed, rocky pillars, distinctly more jagged and rough than the gray, monolithic cliff, come into view from the west side of Brooks Lake, together forming one of the most magnificent panoramas seen on any hike in this guidebook. Like most of the Absaroka Range, these cliffs and buttes were formed from volcanic lava laid down during the Tertiary period, and resemble the formations in the Washakie Wilderness around Wiggins Fork (No's. 28-30).

The trail begins near Brooks Lake Campground, circles the lake to the Brooks Lake Creek Valley, and meanders north to Upper Brooks and Rainbow Lakes, the latter at 4.1 miles. This area serves both as a one-day destination and as a first-night camp for a long backpack trip north through Bear Cub Pass into the Teton Wilderness Area. Wear suitable boots for wading the tributaries around Brooks Lake; take repellent for mosquitoes, especially bad in July; expect commercial horse groups; keep a sharp eye out for moose in the valley. FISH: Rbw 11'', Mcknw 18'', Brk 9'' in Brooks Lake, Brk 10'' in Upper Brooks and Rainbow Lakes.

Drive on U.S. 287 about 23 miles northwest of Dubois to the Brooks Lake Campground turnoff, 7.7 miles southeast of Togwotee Pass.

Turn north onto the dirt road, marked with a sign, and proceed 5.1 miles to the campground access road. Turn right where a new road forks left to the Brooks Lake Lodge and find parking near the lake shore below the campsites.

Pass through the buck fence next to the parking area, cross a small, willow-filled tributary, and follow jeep tracks around the south side of Brooks Lake, bearing toward the massive breccia cliffs on the skyline two miles away. Curve right around the lake on any of the several well-worn horse trails and ford three or four branching tributaries, all shallow but some too wide to jump. Traverse a steeper hillside after 0.7 mile where a range of thick conifers blocks the view of the breccia cliffs left and the vista encompasses the jagged outcroppings of the Pinnacle Buttes east and the cliffs above Bonneville Creek northeast. Maintain elevation above the thick willows around Brooks Lake Creek near 1.2 miles as the trail to Bonneville Pass (No. 26) drops to a crossing, and climb gradually north to the right side of the valley.

Continue up the valley past an old log cabin and corral which shows on the far hillside left and follow a slight ridge between two shallow drainages. Cross the left tributary at 2.0 miles, swing right and soon cross the main branch of Brooks Lake Creek, and make a short, steep climb up a forested hillside. Here the beautiful, gray breccia cliffs can again be seen on the skyline west above a dark range of conifers. The creek drainage from Upper and Lower Jade Lakes marks the hillside below and Brooks Lake Creek shows through the valley ahead. Drop again to treeline after 2.4 miles, continue in and out of trees along the right side of the valley, crossing several tributaries, and after 2.9 miles break to a view of Upper Brooks Lake.

The trail proceeds across two branches of a main creek at 3.1 miles, skirts the east side of the lake, and climbs north-northwest to Bear Cub Pass and the Teton Wilderness boundary at 3.6 miles, marked by signs. Another path — unmarked on the topo but drafted onto the map photo — loops around the north side of Upper Brooks Lake, then stays on the right side of the west tributary and climbs gradually to Rainbow Lake at 4.1 miles. Secluded, hard-ground camping sites can be found near Rainbow Lake or along any of the tributaries of Brooks Lake Creek several hundred yards away from the main trail.

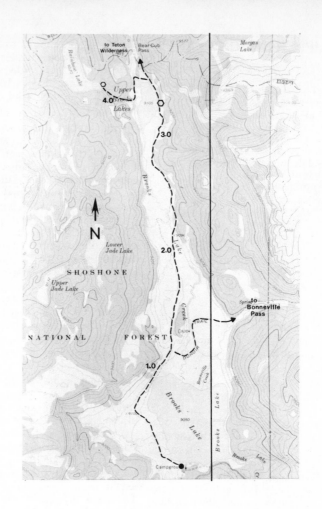

Veteran backpackers at Upper Brooks Lake

Horse packer

26 BONNEVILLE PASS

One day trip or backpack
Distance: 4.5 miles/7.2 KM. one way
Hiking time: 3-3½ hours one way
Elevation gain: 880 feet/268 M.
Maximum elevation: 9,960 feet/3,036 M.
Season: Mid-July through September
Topographic maps:
   U.S.G.S. Togwotee Pass, Wyo. 1965
   U.S.G.S. Dundee Meadows, Wyo. 1956
Wind River Ranger District
Shoshone National Forest

Bonneville Pass memorializes Benjamin Louis Eulalie de Bonneville, army officer, fur trader, and adventurer, who in 1832 led a historic expedition of 110 men and twenty wagons west along the Platte River through South Pass to the Green River. In September 1833 he made the first ascent of Gannett Peak in the Wind River Range, according to Orrin H. Bonney in his *Guide To The Wyoming Mountains*. Bonneville furnished detailed journals and careful maps of his travels to Washington Irving who embellished the story in his classic work, *The Adventures of Captain Bonneville*. The DuNoir Trail to Bonneville Pass can be intercepted either from a new, and usually dry, trail east of Brooks Lake (see map) or from the trail to Upper Brooks Lake (No. 25), a wet but very scenic route, described below.

Drive on U.S. 287 about 23 miles northwest of Dubois to the Brooks Lake Campground turnoff, 7.7 miles southeast of Togwotee Pass. Turn north onto the dirt road (slick and rutted after rainstorms) and proceed 4.2 miles to a right fork marked "Dead End 1." Either find off-the-road parking here or continue another 0.9 mile to the Brooks Lake Campground, fork right where a new road goes to the Brooks Lake Lodge, and park near the lake shore below the campsites.

From the parking area near the lake shore pass through the nearby buck fence, jump across a willow-filled tributary and begin circling the south side of Brooks Lake on jeep tracks. Ahead, a magnificent, gray cliff of breccia rock, over 10,800 feet in elevation and streaked with horizontal bands, looms into the skyline; behind, the Pinnacle Buttes, equally high but jagged and creviced, show occasionally through the trees. Curve right around the lake on any of several, well-worn horse trails, wading the many rivulets that wash the lake bowl. Drop over a slight rise above the north end of the lake and fork right onto the DuNoir Trail after 1.2 miles where the trail to Upper Brooks Lakes (No. 25) continues left up the valley.

Follow the main path of the Dunoir Trail east-northeast through several hundred yards of thick willows, wading the 20-foot-wide Brooks Lake Creek. Enter the Bonneville Creek Valley between the massive Pinnacle Buttes right and the unnamed, 12,681-foot cliffs left and begin a rolling climb in and out of limber pine up the left side of the valley. Curve east after 2.2 miles, passing a meadow which opens to the left. Wind on a hillside contour through clumps of tall spruce, eventually climb through a post-and-pole gate, then pass clear-cut hillsides of slash and down timber across the creek and swing right over a main tributary after 2.7 miles. Continue across several more tributaries and break onto an open hillside at 3.5 miles which gives an unobstructed view south of the spectacular Jules Bowl. A flat-topped cliff wall, often snow-covered through August, shapes the middle of the amphitheater and sharp spires of the Pinnacle Buttes rim the right and left sides.

Proceed on a more noticeable climb up the valley, loop right then left across a cascading creek at 3.7 miles, and after another one-half mile of rolling climb through pine and spruce enter the open saddle of Bonneville Pass. Swing right across the small Bonneville Creek at mile 4.2, pick up the trail 20 yards or so below treeline on the east side of the pass, and continue to a dainty tarn at 4.7 miles which spills into Dundee Creek. From the grassy saddle here — a pleasant stopping point — the view opens at 8°/NNE toward nearby rock pillars of the Continental Divide north of Dundee Meadows, and then extends at 220°/WSW toward blue, horizon mountains in the Teton National Forest. The DuNoir Trail drops east from Bonneville Pass, enters the Dundee Meadows after 6.0 miles, and comes to a junction at mile 6.8 where the Kisinger Lakes Trail splits south to Basin Creek Meadows and Kisinger Lakes.

Pinnacle Buttes beyond Brooks Lake

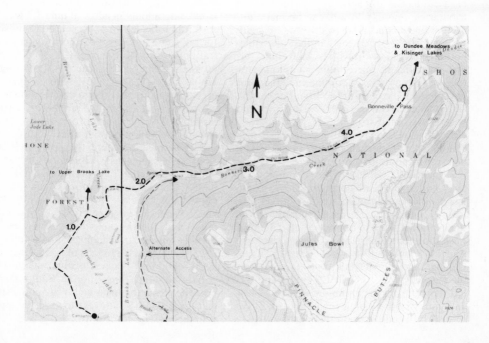

27 FIVE POCKETS

Backpack
Distance: 7.0 miles/11.3 KM. one way
Hiking time: 4½ hours one way
Elevation gain: 1,110 feet/338 M.
Elevation loss: 700 feet/312 M.
Maximum elevation: 8,810 feet/2,685 M.
Season: Mid-June through early October
Topographic maps:
  U.S.G.S. Indian Point, Wyo. 1956
  U.S.G.S. Ramshorn Peak, Wyo. 1956
  U.S.G.S. Five Pockets, Wyo. 1956
Wind River Ranger District
Shoshone National Forest

From a glance at the topo map, the unique Five Pockets formation in the southwest corner of the Washakie Wilderness appears as a mammoth paw print, with five, linked valleys or "pockets" forming the toes. Spectacular, glacier-cut ridges rise between the valley into high bluffs, composed of the same volcanic breccia as found in the Frontier Creek/Wiggins Fork area (No's. 28-30). Both valley bottoms and ridgetops make exciting routes for cross-country exploring, and from a base camp near any of the many Horse Creek tributaries, one-day forays can be made into each of the pockets. Use trails, broken mostly by horse packers, run the length of the valley bottoms; Lake Pocket with its high alpine tarn and magnificent, surrounding amphitheater, receives the most use; commercial dude outfits often have camps in the Five Pockets basin. Boedeker Butte, southeast of Five Pockets, was named from the historic photo of Harold Boedeker, Dubois homesteader, standing next to his bagged bighorn sheep beneath that monolithic rock tower.

Drive on U.S. 26/287 to the middle of Dubois and proceed north on Horse Creek Road. Stay on the main road — gravel after about 5 miles — across a cattleguard marking the National Forest boundary at 9.3 miles. Pass turnoffs to the Horse Creek Guard Station at mile 10.5 and Horse Creek Campground at mile 10.9, then stay right past the Parque Creek Road at 12.5 miles and fork left (north) from the Double Cabin Road near 13.0 miles where a sign reads "Horse Creek Trail." Proceed north on this narrow road —

drafted onto the map — as far as condition permit, coming to a sign reading "Hors Creek Trail" after 3.3 miles.

Hike northwest up the road, passing a view of the green-roofed T-Cross Ranch cabins a 204°/SW across the Horse Creek Valley Cross a tributary at 0.2 mile and climb a sligh rise to a beautiful view of bluffs of rocky strat that comprise the Elkhorn Ridge at 46°/ENI and the rounded outcroppings of The Ram shorn at 300°/NW. Come to a sign for moto closure and a sign reading "3 Horse Cree Trail," follow the path into aspen and pine a 7°/N, soon dip across a tributary from the righ and swing around a marshy area (left) with pond at the far end. Cross a sage hillside afte 0.8 mile, turn right where a trail joins from th left, eventually cross another tributary abov the bridge and enter a glen of aspen, crosse by an old buck fence. Continue northwest int tall, red-barked lodgepole pine, passing a tra register; pass a second, then a third grass glen, and after 2.0 miles break into th meadow surrounding Carson Lake. Here th view again extends northwest to the beautifu outcroppings of The Ramshorn.

Penetrate the narrow valley opening a 319°/NNW from Carson Lake, drop the climb, and cross a sage hillside at 2.8 miles Continue along a grassy drainage to a lookou of Horse Creek west and of the 11,316-foo high point of The Ramshorn at 274°/WNW Break into a long meadow at mile 3.7 where spur trail forks left to a "Reserved Campsite for big game hunters, bear north on the mai trail toward the lofty spire of Cathedral Pea on the skyline, and come to a crossing c Horse Creek at 4.4 miles. After wading th creek, climb gradually into conifers along th west valleyside, cross two branches of a tribu tary near 5.0 miles, and drop past two pond toward the valley bottom after 5.5 miles. (I the open meadow here the Twilight Cree Trail forks right (east), climbs north past th magnificent Cathedral Peak Range, and even tually connects with Frontier Creek (No. 28 via Cougar Creek.) To proceed to Five Poc kets, wade the smaller Horse Creek at 5. miles and follow the valley northwest fo another mile or so, reaching a good vantage c the three northerly pockets of Lake, Bear, an West. Hidden Pocket opens beyond th conifer-covered range north; South Pocke branches from the main valley in another mil and leads south-southwest toward the alpin summits of The Ramshorn.

Bluffs above Horse Creek Valley

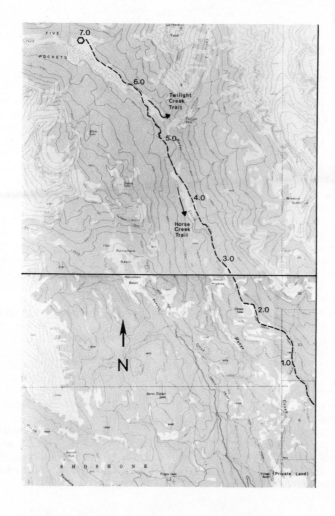

28 FRONTIER CREEK

Backpack
Distances:
  Canyon Creek - 4.7 miles/7.6 KM.
  Cougar Pass Trail - 6.9 miles/11.1 KM.
  Petrified Forest - 8.0 miles/12.9 KM.
Hiking time: 5-5½ hours one way
Elevation gain: 1,160 feet/354 M.
Maximum elevation: 9,240 feet/2,816 M.
Season: July through September
Topographic maps:
  U.S.G.S. Snow Lake, Wyo. 1956
  U.S.G.S. Emerald Lake, Wyo. 1956
Wind River Ranger District
Shoshone National Forest

Majestic, pillared bluffs, thousand-foot vertical cliffs, rock-strewn rivulets, and unexplored canyons characterize the Washakie Wilderness in the Absaroka Range, a region that has been called the most rugged and sublime in the United States. The shadowed, creviced breccia walls here contrast sharply from the sharp peaktops in the Wind River and Salt River Ranges and also from the rolling summits of the Gros Ventre Range. And the trail system, although less extensive, provides a recommended alternative to the tourist-jammed pathways of the Fitzpatrick, Bridger, and Popo Agie Wildernesses. This Wilderness, named in memory of the respected Chief Washakie of the Shosones, was established in 1972 from the existing South Absaroka Wilderness and Stratified Primitive Area.

The Frontier Creek Trail begins north of Double Cabin Campground and crosses four branches of Frontier Creek — cold and knee-deep through early August — to the Double Cabin. Wading shoes make this crossing and the subsequent crossings at 4.7 and 5.9 miles much more tolerable. The historic log hut called Double Cabin, now nearly gone, received its name when two fur trappers "holed up" there for winter, sometime in the mid-1880's. Stricken with a bad case of cabin fever, they started feuding and finally marked a line down the middle of the cabin. Its meaning was clear: "Cross this line an' yo' daid!" Thus, in the desperate circumstances of a long and dark winter, the trappers made a "double cabin" out of their cramped, one-room dwelling.

Drive on U.S. 26/287 to the middle of Dubois and proceed north on Horse Creek Road. (The pavement ends after about 5 miles but the gravel road is passable by sedans, except possibly after heavy rains.) Stay right after 10.5 miles where a road forks left to the Horse Creek Guard Station, stay right again after 12.5 miles where the Parque Creek Road forks left, and continue over rough road to the Double Cabin Campground, a total of 25.6 miles from U.S. 26/287. Parking for backpackers is available in the open flat north of the campground.

From the "Frontier Creek Petrified Forest" sign where spectacular Norton Point shows a 352°/N, bear northeast across Frontier Creek and follow a jeep trail inside treeline to a sign reading "Cougar Pass Trail," etc. Angle left onto a single path and proceed through rolling pine-covered terrain up the Frontier Creek Valley, keeping track of the main tributary valleys west of Frontier Creek to determine progress. Cross a rock-lined rivulet and a smaller drainage after 1.1 miles, traverse a steep hillside near mile 1.8, then pick up a tributary filled with deadfall (left) and bend left across it at 2.9 miles. Fork left toward Frontier Creek where a right fork enters an eroded wash, contour across a plateau to a tributary crossing at mile 3.5, and soon break out of conifers to marshes and meadows. Near 4.0 miles pass a vista of the "10285" ridgetop at 232°/WSW, continue across several tributaries, then swing left through a meadow to a crossing of Frontier Creek at 4.7 miles. In view at this point is the Canyon Creek Valley, the fifth main valley west of Frontier Creek from the trailhead.

Recross Frontier Creek at mile 5.9, wind past deeply eroded washes and come to a view of a snowy amphitheater wall (left) near 6.9 miles above the Cougar Creek Valley. (Here the unsigned Cougar Creek Trail turns west across Frontier Creek, penetrates Cougar Pass in another 3.6 miles, and connects with the Twilight Creek Trail (see No. 27)). On the Frontier Creek Trail dip through a 20-foot ravine at 7.3 miles where cascades spill through the eroded volcanic rock above. Pass through open parks and hillsides — in bloom through mid-summer with beautiful wildflowers — and continue across more deeply-cut tributaries near 8.0 miles and beyond. Colorful chips of petrified wood, **not to be removed from the Wilderness Area,** show through the sparkling water of these creeks and litter the surrounding hillsides.

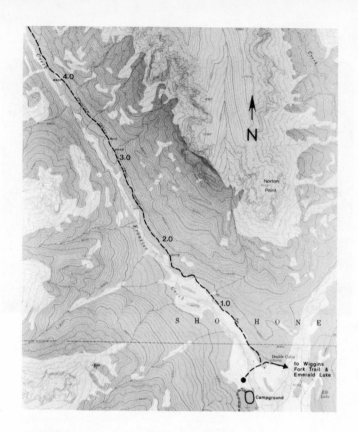

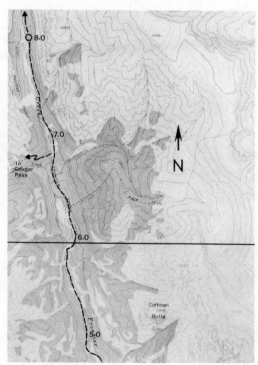

Petrified tree trunk

Norton Point beyond trailhead sign

29 EMERALD LAKE

Backpack
Distances: (from Double Cabin trailhead)
  Fire Creek - 3.2 miles/5.2 KM.
  Emerald Lake Trail - 5.2 miles/8.4 KM.
  Emerald Lake - 12.0 miles/19.3 KM.
Hiking time: 7-8 hours one way
Elevation gain: 2,820 feet/860 M.
Elevation loss: 220 feet/67 M.
Maximum elevation: 10,680 feet/3,255 M.
Season: July through September
Topographic maps:
  U.S.G.S. Snow Lake, Wyo. 1956
  U.S.G.S. Emerald Lake, Wyo. 1956
Wind River Ranger District
Shoshone National Forest

During the Oligocene Period some 30 to 40 million years ago a primeval forest of giant pine and cedar, some 15 feet in diameter and possibly 200 feet tall, covered much of the Wiggins Fork area. Volcanic action eventually buried this forest under hundreds of feet of lava and volcanic debris, and subsequent rivers and glaciers carved new cliffs and valleys from the rock. In the process, the remains of the ancient forest were exposed, now sculptured in petrified wood. A major attraction to the Wiggins Fork area has always been these beautiful samples of "Wyoming agate," petrified wood, and other colorful stones found along the streambeds. Below Double Cabin Campground, rockhounds constantly comb the sandbars and brave the icy waters in search of gems. **NOTE: In order to preserve the natural state of the Wilderness Area, the Forest Service prohibits rock hunting within the Wilderness boundaries. Maximum sentence: $500 and/or 6 months in jail. The collection of incidental samples which wash downstream each year is permitted.**

Nine major creek crossings—each chilling and uncomfortably swift through mid-August —make the hike to Emerald Lake one of the wettest in this guide. As with the hikes up Frontier Creek (No. 28) and Wiggins Fork (No. 30), wading shoes are recommended equipment. Majestic buttes and interesting volcanic rock, exquisite, pristine Emerald Lake, unspoiled habitat for bighorn sheep, moose, and bear all make a trip through the Emerald Creek Valley truly exciting.

Drive from Dubois to the Double Cabin Campground via Horse Creek Road, following the directions given for the Frontier Creek hike (No. 28).

Cross the four branches of Frontier Creek, turn right where the sign reads "Wiggins Fork Trail ½," then pass the Wilderness Guard Station and bear 98°/ESE to Wiggins Fork at 0.5 mile. Cross the two branches of Wiggins Fork and an unnamed tributary and follow an easterly bearing through open pine until intercepting the Wiggins Fork Trail near 0.9 mile. Turn north-northeast on any of the cow paths or jeep trails, pick up the blazed trail in another 200 yards or so, and after mile 1.2 break from the pine to an opening with the trail register. Wind northeast past scattered snags from the 1952 Wiggins Fork Fire, cross a 15-yard-long rocky tributary at 1.4 miles and contour along a forested ledge above Wiggins Fork to a fire-burned hilltop near mile 1.7. Loop through a small tributary at 2.3 miles and continue up the valley to the 20-yard long, rock-filled Fire Creek tributary at mile 3.2, marked by sign and opposite the Snow Lake Creek Valley.

Drop closer to Wiggins Fork, continue on a rolling hillside traverse, cross Wiggins Fork at mile 4.6 and recross it at mile 4.8. Bear north-northeast through tall pine and spruce to a third crossing after 5.2 miles where Wiggins Fork turns east. Here the Emerald Lake Trail, marked by a sign north of the crossing, proceeds straight while the Wiggins Fork Trail (No. 30) turns east toward Burwell Pass and the Caldwell Trail. Follow the Emerald Lake Trail on a northerly bearing into the narrow valley; cross the rocky bed and cold waters of Emerald Creek at mile 5.9, again at mile 6.4, and then again at mile 6.9. Continue on a rolling climb through spruce and fir up the southwest valleyside, pass lookouts of the prominent Sheep Creek Valley north after 7.6 miles, and contour along the northeasterly reaches of Crescent Top Mountain. Cross two main avalanche paths after 8.5 miles, climb steadily to a crossing at 8.8 miles of the tributary that flows down from the Devils Graveyard, and wind across avalanche paths and gullies at miles 9.2, 9.4, 9.5, and 9.8. Make a final crossing of Emerald Creek at 10.3 miles to the east side the valley, bear north along game trails through scattered conifers, then break from trees near 11.4 miles and climb steeply to the Emerald Lake plateau at 12.0 miles.

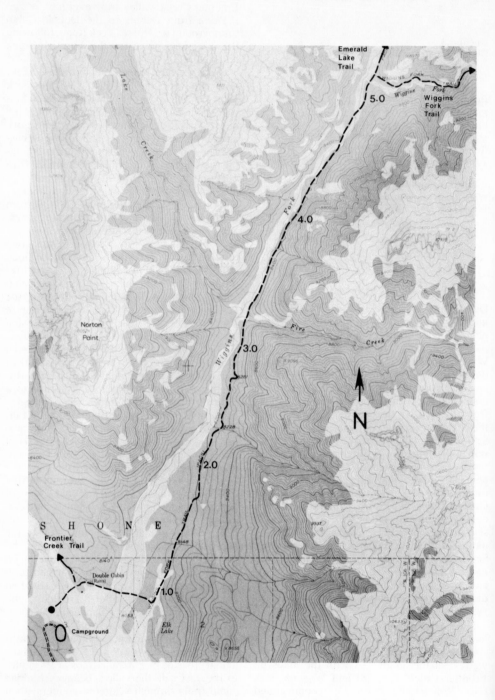

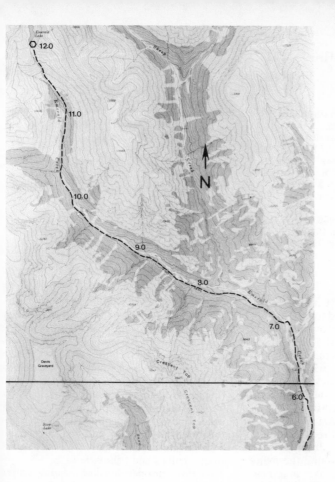

Eroded landscape in Emerald Valley

30 WIGGINS FORK

Backpack
Distances: (from Double Cabin trailhead)
  Fire Creek - 3.2 miles/5.2 KM.
  Emerald Lake Trail - 5.2 miles/8.4 KM.
  Caldwell Trail - 11.0 miles/17.7 KM.
Hiking time: 7-7½ hours one way
Elevation gain: 1,780 feet/543 M.
Maximum elevation: 9,860 feet/3,005 M.
Season: July through September
Topographic maps:
  U.S.G.S. Snow Lake, Wyo. 1956
  U.S.G.S. Wiggins Peak, Wyo. 1969
  U.S.G.S. Mount Burwell, Wyo. 1969
Wind River Ranger District
Shoshone National Forest

Like the trails along Frontier Creek (No. 28) and Emerald Creek to Emerald Lake (No. 29), the Wiggins Fork Trail still enjoys a precious isolation from hordes of tourists, due for the most part to the ruggedness of the terrain. But for veteran backpackers, this trip will prove unforgettable. High, scenic rock-and-conifer bluffs rise steeply above either side of the trail, reinforcing the feeling of seclusion. Tons of rounded river rock and jackstraw piles of deadwood fill Wiggins Fork Creek in infinite variation. And deeply-cut gullies, washed with each spring's thaw, surround the many splashing tributaries. From a base camp near the Emerald Lake Trail junction at 5.2 miles, the upper valley of the Wiggins Fork, with its steep but intriguing side drainages, can be explored on a one-day trip. This camping site also gives good access into the Emerald Creek Valley (see No. 29). Or, an exciting three- or four-day trip can be routed by looping southeast from the Wiggins Fork Trail over Caldwell Pass and continuing southwest through the less-explored Black and Brown Rock Canyons.

Drive from Dubois to the Double Cabin Campground via Horse Creek Road, following the directions given for the Frontier Creek hike (No. 28).

First, hike from the trailhead near Double Cabin Campground to the Wiggins Fork Trail turnoff at mile 5.2, using the directions in Emerald Lake (No. 29). Fork east onto the Wiggins Fork Trail where the Emerald Lake Trail proceeds north, and continue in and out of trees to another crossing of Wiggins Fork Trail at 5.7 miles where the view extends

downstream to the beautiful, gray rock columns of Crescent Top. Pick up a tributary (left) which splits from Wiggins Fork, swing left across it about 100 yards above the confluence at mile 6.2, then climb southeast through four, short switchbacks and follow a rolling contour through mixed conifers. Drop then swing right to another tributary crossing after 6.9 miles, resume the rolling hillside contour northeast above Wiggins Fork (left), and continue through cool limber pine and Engelmann spruce for another two miles, crossing a series of rocky gullies and tributaries.

Pass through open hillside meadows after 9.3 miles where hunting campsites have been located. Make a final crossing over Wiggins Fork at mile 9.7 and contour along the south-facing hillside, soon entering alpine meadows with views east of the grassy skyline range. Behind on a 210°/SW bearing are the high cliffs and rocky, volcanic buttes which cradle the Wiggins Fork Creek, a distinct contrast to the view ahead. Cross a dry, rocky gully at 10.5 miles, marked as a spring tributary on the U.S.G.S. topo. Bear 44°/ENE across the open hillside and come to a signed junction with the Caldwell Trail at 11.0 miles. From this point the Wiggins Fork Trail continues north on a switchbacking climb to Burwell Pass, then drops through the Cow Creek drainage to a junction with the Greybull River Trail. The Caldwell Trail, identified as the Absaroka Trail on the topo, curves southeast above the Wiggins Fork Valley to the Caldwell Creek Vally and loops southwest through Black and Brown Rock Canyons to an eventual meeting with Wiggins Fork three miles below Double Cabin Campground.

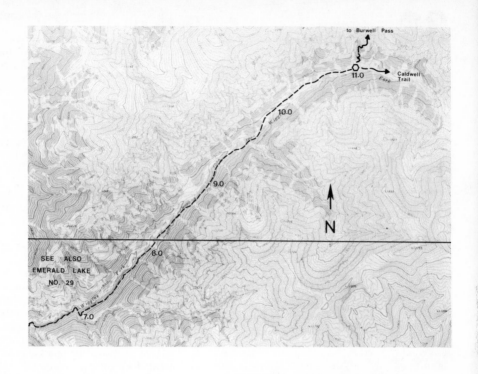

Trail fork nap

31 ROSS LAKE

One day trip or back pack
Distances:
  Whiskey Mtn. Tr. - 2.9 miles/4.7 KM.
  Ross Lake Trail - 4.9 miles/7.9 KM.
  Ross Lake - 6.1 miles/9.8 KM.
Hiking time: 4½-5 hours one way
Elevation gain: 3,030 feet/924 M.
Elevation loss: 915 feet/279 M.
Maximum elevation: 10,320 feet/3,146 M.
Season: Mid-June through early October
Topographic maps:
  U.S.G.S. Torrey Lake, Wyo. 1968
  U.S.G.S. Simpson Lake, Wyo. 1968
Wind River Ranger District
Shoshone National Forest

On September 27, 1976 the United States Congress passed a resolution designating the historic Glacier Primitive Area in the Shoshone National Forest "as the 'Fitzpatrick Wilderness' and, therefore, as a component of the National Wilderness Preservation System." The name honors Thomas Fitzpatrick, mountainman, fur trader, guide and partner of Jim Bridger after whom the Bridger Wilderness is named. One of the most exciting destinations in the Fitzpatrick is two-mile-long Ross Lake, ensconced in an enormous, glacier-polished chasm with 2,000-foot granite walls. The rock barriers make lakeside travel very tough going, if not impossible; the best way to explore this beautiful valley and to get to Upper Ross Lake is with a portable raft. Both lakes are named for Nellie Tayloe Ross, Wyoming governor in 1925-7 and the first woman governor of any state. FISH: Rbw 13''-21'', Rbw/Ct X's in Ross Lake; Ct 12'' in Upper Ross Lake; none in the tributary lakes west and south.

Drive on U.S. 26/287 to the Fitzpatrick Wilderness access road southeast of Dubois and proceed to the Glacier Trail parking loop, following the driving instructions in Lake Louise (No. 32).

Begin from the trailhead register north of the parking loop and hike southwest to a sign reading "Whiskey Mountain Trail/Simpson Lake Trail 5'' inside the barbed wire fence. Fork right at 0.5 mile where the signed Lake Louise Trail (No. 32) turns left toward the West Torrey Creek Valley and climb steadily west on the winding path toward salmon-colored bluffs on the skyline. Cross through conifers and over a small tributary — nearly dry by mid-summer — at 0.7 mile, continue the steep climb up the sage-covered Whiskey mountainside via several long switchbacks, and come to expansive lookouts of the Torrey Creek Valley near 1.1 mile. Smooth, glacial-polished granite knobs shine in the sun on the south valleyside, and the black snags from the 1976 forest fire show farther west above unseen Lake Louise.

Leave the sage and cedar trees after 1.3 miles and traverse west past rocky talus and into thicker conifers. Cross a small tributary, loop right (north) above the drainageway at mile 2.1 where the view extends south to the high Glacier Trail, and soon bend west again into the trees. Climb on an easier grade after passing through a broken-down barbed wire fence, cross a second small rivulet at 2.7 miles, and break to a high, ridgeline climb in 200 more yards, a windy but very scenic bivouac site. In view at 190°/SSW are the shimmering waters of Hidden Lake, marked on its northeast side by a white-water outlet. And beneath the skyline formed by Ram Flat, four unnamed glaciers — the largest at 200°/SW — cling to the rugged, shaded hillside beyond still-hidden Ross Lake.

Follow the faint trail west onto an alpine hillside: do not fork left onto a use trail but climb gradually via the right fork toward a slight opening in the trees ahead. (The unmarked Whiskey Mountain Trail climbs right (northwest) up the alpine hillside.) Look for cairns after 3.1 miles as the trail passes a viewpoint of Ross Lake and drops slightly south-southwest through clumps of conifers, some blackened by fire. Enter an open flat near mile 3.9 where interesting jumbles of boulders cover the hillside right. Stay near treeline, passing a small pond (far right) at 4.8 miles, and pick up the Ross Lake Trail just inside treeline. Wind south across the ridgetop, descend quickly after mile 5.1 through many small switchbacks — a point which gives view to the south end of Ross Lake — and contour at 198°/SW over a well-blazed trail beneath the hillside right. Drop steadily again after 5.7 miles through rocks and scattered pine until reaching the northern tip of Ross Lake at 6.1 miles.

Ross Lake

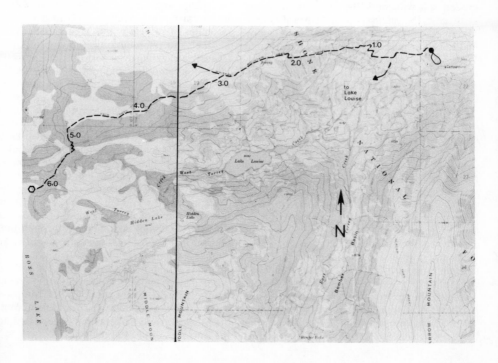

32 LAKE LOUISE

One day trip or backpack
Distance: 2.7 miles/4.3 KM. one way
Hiking time: 2 hours one way
Elevation gain: 1,160 feet/354 M.
Elevation loss: 320 feet/98 M.
Maximum elevation: 8,520 feet/2,597 M.
Season: Mid-June through early October
Topographic map:
  U.S.G.S. Torrey Lake, Wyo. 1968
Wind River Ranger District
Shoshone National Forest

On July 8, 1976 a campfire near Lake Louise crept through the rocks of its fire ring and started a forest fire which burned for four days, ravaging over 1,650 acres of a beautiful area in the northern Wind River Range. Sudden, whipping winds and tinder-dry duff for ground cover makes the Lake Louise bowl extremely susceptible to forest fire. **Thus, the use of backpacking stoves is highly recommended.** Although blackened snags and eroded soil will mark the hillsides for many years now, the glacial-polished cliffs of Middle Mountain, the granite boulders—many marked with glacial striae—which surround West Torrey Creek, and the general ruggedness of the terrain make this hike well-worthwhile. FISH: Brk 10'', Rbw ll'' in Lake Louise, Ct 12'', Rbw 12'' in Hidden Lake.

From Dubois (1st and Ramshorn intersection) drive southeast on U.S. 26/287 for 3.9 miles to the Fitzpatrick Wilderness access road, marked with a "Wyo. Game & Fish Commission" sign. Turn south onto the gravel road, soon fork left across a cattleguard toward Torrey Creek Lakes, and fork left again after 2.5 miles. Stay on the main road through three miles of private land, pass west of Torrey, Ring, and Trail Lakes, then fork right around the Trail Lake Ranch after almost 8.0 miles and continue to the large Glacier Trail parking loop, a total of 9.4 miles from U.S. 26/287.

Begin hiking from the trailhead register north of the parking loop, pass a sign reading "Whiskey Mountain Trail," etc. inside the barbed wire fence, and follow the path south-west and west through sagebrush. Fork left at the signed Louise Lake Trail turnoff after 0.5 mile, wind through fragrant cedar, limber pine, Engelmann spruce and Douglas fir to a crossing of a swampy tributary at 0.7 mile, then climb steadily west and south, and stay right at mile 1.0 where the left fork drops to a new bridge over Torrey Creek, the Glacier Trail access (No. 33). Climb steeply west-southwest up a ridge and soon swing left out of scattered trees to a pleasing panorama. The rock-lined East Torrey Creek Valley—also called Bomber Basin after a World War II trainer plane crashed and started a forest fire there in 1942—opens to the south, a knob east of Middle Mountain filled with blackened snags marks the 1976 fire, and the West Torrey Creek canyon shows southwest.

Drop through a basin with a fire-scarred campsite at 1.0 mile (where the trail ends on the U.S.G.S. topo), proceed on the well-worn path past a balanced rock (right), then follow cairns past white-water cascades in the creek (left) and cross a root-entwined tributary at mile 1.6. Continue the climb through a gulch and past a meadow filled with dead trees, then drop right around a small knoll and traverse along the rocky trail to an open, grassy flat and tributary crossing at 1.9 miles. Swing left toward West Torrey Creek and pass 20 yards of beautiful, splashing cascades, then follow more cairns on a rocky climb to a view of cascades just below the lake outlet. With another short scramble up the granite knoll, come to a dazzling overlook of Lake Louise. A large log jam fills the outlet of the lake, glacial-scrubbed rock outcroppings and conifer clumps line the lake bowl and three glaciers gleam with sun from the east side of Shale Mountain at 244°/W.

Cross carefully over the logs at the outlet at 2.3 miles, circle the east extension of the lake, and after climbing over a rocky rise come to several campsites above the shore near 2.7 miles, as figured for the information capsule. To continue to Hidden Lake — a difficult hike-and-climb of another 2 miles — follow the use trail over rock mounds and through fire-charred conifers along the south side of Lake Louise. Climb over gray, lichen-covered boulders which fill the inlet, follow unofficial cairns above and left of West Torrey Creek, then eventually swing south (on the Simpson Lake topo) toward the bare rock cliffs of Middle Mountain and make a final, steep climb to the northeast end of Hidden Lake.

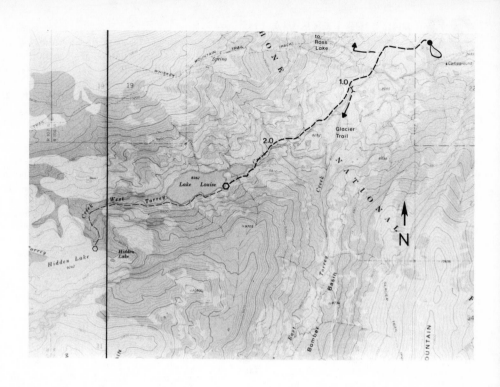

Rock-enclosed Lake Louise

33 PHILLIPS LAKE VIA THE GLACIER TRAIL

Backpack
Distances:
  Dinwoody Trail - 9.8 miles/15.8 KM.
  Phillips Lake - 10.5 miles/16.9 KM.
Hiking time: 6-7 hours one way
Elevation gain: 3,945 feet/1,202 M.
Elevation loss: 1,365 feet/416 M.
Maximum elevation: 10,895 feet/3,321 M.
Season: July through September
Topographic maps:
  U.S.G.S. Torrey Lake, Wyo. 1968
  U.S.G.S. Ink Wells, Wyo. 1968
Wind River Ranger District
Shoshone National Forest

Like the faithful on a pilgrimage to Mecca, mountain climbers come from all over the United States and around the world to walk the historic Glacier Trail and pay homage to 13,804-foot, glacier-clad Gannett Peak, highest point in Wyoming. Unfortunately, the Glacier-Trail-to-Gannet-Peak trip is often listed in where-to-go checklists as **the** backpack route for Wyoming. This misinformed, token representation results in heavy overuse: Hillsides *en route* are a severely "trailed" or rutted as on the Pole Creek Trail to Seneca Lake (No. 41), backpackers as profuse as on the Big Sandy Trail to Big Sandy Lake and Lonesome Lake/Cirque of the Towers (No. 50). But for veteran hikers, with at least 8 to 10 days for the trip, the ethereal world of glacier-snow and granite-rock and the incomparable vistas around Gannett Peak provide compensation for the long, tough trip in.

In October 1976, a large landslide occurred above the Torrey Creek campgrounds and resulted in the construction of a new parking area and bridge over Torrey Creek (see map). The text below begins from the new Torrey Creek Entrance and charts the course to Phillips Lake at mile 10.5, the first of the Dinwoody Lakes and a common first-day's goal. And the Big Meadows hike (No. 34) continues from Phillips Lake past Downs Fork Valley to Big Meadows at mile 18.0, a possible second-day's destination.

Drive on U.S. 26/287 to the Fitzpatrick Wilderness access road southeast of Dubois and proceed to the Glacier Trail parking loop, following the driving instructions in the Lake Louise hike (No. 32).

Pick up the Glacier Trail/Lake Louise Trail north of the parking loop and proceed southwest to the Glacier Trail turnoff at mile 1.0, as described in No. 32. Swing left (east) across the new 50-foot bridge over Torrey Creek, climb gradually south up the East Torrey Creek Valley, then swing left after 2.2 miles and make a switchbacking climb to the Bomber Basin Trail at 2.7 miles. Climb northeast to a slight ridge at mile 3.0 where the view extends to 11,151-foot Whiskey Mountain at 288°/WNW and to rounded, glacier-polished knobs in West Torrey Creek below. Drop to the old Glacier Trail at 3.5 miles beyond a small tributary and climb south through long switchbacks, with an occasional screened view of the three glaciers beyond East Torrey Creek at 234°/WSW.

After 4.1 miles break from the last conifer clump to a long traverse southwest over the alpine hillsides of Arrow Mountain. Pass through a shady nook of trees — a nice rest spot — near 4.9 miles, break to a view of a sharp, rocky mountain at 171°/S which rises above East Torrey Creek, and climb steadily up the alpine tundra where the trail shows ahead for a half-mile. Pass over a slight rise at mile 6.7 which gives view to rock outcroppings (right) and to the Williamson Corral ruins farther down. Drop by branches of an east Torrey Creek tributary (possibly contaminated by cattle) and climb gradually south to the "10895" saddle at 8.4 miles. Now in view are the magnificent rock walls of Dinwoody Lakes amphitheater at 176°/SSW, often laced with snow. Long Horse Ridge can be seen also on the distant skyline, highest at 165°/S near Fourts Horn about 9 miles away.

Curve left on a drop around the willows of Burro Flat, cross a muddy tributary near 9.2 miles, and stay south at mile 9.8 where the signed Dinwoody Trail turns east. (The Dinwoody Trail stays high above Dinwoody Creek Valley (south) and bears east for 6.5 miles to the Wind River Indian Reservation.) Cross Burro Flat Creek at mile 9.9 — the first clear, safe water of the trip — then descend south into fragrant pine, swing right over a bridged tributary and follow the rocky path to Phillips Lake at mile 10.5. (A use trail follows Phillips Creek north and west for 0.4 mile to larger Upper Phillips Lake, then proceeds south of the inlet on a steep climb to secluded, timberline Golden Lake.) Continue with No. 34.

82

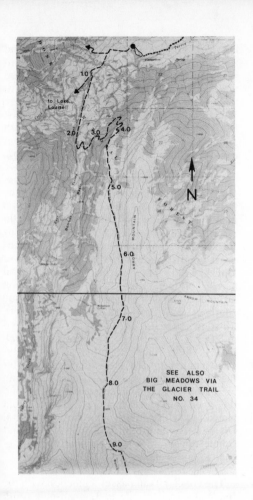

Sun-splashed waterfall

34 BIG MEADOWS VIA THE GLACIER TRAIL

Distances: (from the Glacier Trailhead)
Double Lake - 11.2 miles/18.0 KM.
Star Lake - 12.2 miles/19.6 KM.
Honeymoon Lake - 13.4 miles/21.6 KM.
Downs Fork Trail - 15.8 miles/25.4 KM.
Big Meadows - 18.0 miles/29.0 KM.
Hiking time: (from Phillips Lake)
5-6 hours one way
Elevation gain: 880 feet/268 M.
Elevation loss: 420 feet/128 M.
Maximum elevation: 10,330 feet/3,149 M.

To continue from Phillips Lake via the Glacier Trail, cross the bridged outlet southeast of the lake at 10.6 miles, climb slightly then switchback left in several more yards. Soon bend south-southeast and drop steadily toward Double Lake, in view ahead through the trees. Step stones over the Double Lake outlet at 11.1 miles, swing right along the rocky lake shore, and come to a spectacular vista of the glacier-carved amphitheater west, divided by a huge rock fortress north of unseen Florence Lake. Pass the south half of Double Lake, cross the cascading inlet near 11.7 miles, then climb through switchbacks to a bridged crossing over Double Lake Creek at 11.9 miles and continue the southerly contour to the west side of Star Lake at mile 12.2.

Wind in and out of pine through rocky terrain, eventually gaining a view of the granite range (right). Wade Honeymoon Creek past willows and mountain bluebell at 12.9 miles, drop gradually along the creek (left) to another crossing near mile 13.2 and in several more yards come to a lookout of Honeymoon Lake. The blue, shadowed canyon walls of Horse Ridge show also from this point and lead right toward the rocky tip of a peak at 181°/SSW, possibly East Sentinel Peak or Mount Warren near Dinwoody Glacier. Proceed through switchbacks on a drop to Honeymoon Lake at 13.4 miles, descend steadily down the Honeymoon Creek Valley to a creek crossing at mile 14.5 and soon come to a trail fork. (Here a

left fork recrosses Honeymoon Creek and leads northeast for 0.5 mile to beautiful, sun-splashed Honeymoon Falls.) Switchback up to a slight saddle after 14.9 miles, then drop to the north end of willow-filled Down Fork Meadows. (A cross-country route loops east here, follows a tributary east, and loops south to the little-explored North Ink Wells Lake, an excellent sidetrip of about 1.3 miles, see map.)

Bear southwest above the wide openings of Downs Fork Meadows, skirt rock-and-pine hillsides (right), and come to a trail junction near mile 15.8. The right fork proceeds southwest and west over level terrain into Downs Fork Valley, then turns northwest and climbs cross-country for another half-mile to Lower Downs Lake. Stay left on the Glacier Trail across bridged Downs Fork Creek, loop around a small knob (left), and continue southeast past the south end of Downs Fork Meadows toward Dinwoody Creek at 16.4 miles. Zig-zag through the Dinwoody Creek Valley; loop right around a steep, rocky-strewn mountainside after 17.2 miles and enter the Big Meadows near 17.8 miles. Here an incredibly beautiful panorama unfolds beyond the open parks: High spires, creviced and blanketed with snow, shape the Continental Divide between Mount Woodrow Wilson and Gannett Peak at 199°/SW, framed by the rugged canyon walls beneath Horse Ridge.

The Glacier Trail passes a junction with the Ink Wells Trail at mile 19.3, a half-mile south of Big Meadows. The Ink Wells Trail crosses Dinwoody Creek and bears northwest beneath Horse Ridge to Echo Lake at 1.4 miles and South Ink Wells Lake at 3.0 miles. Then it crosses Horse Ridge at Scenic Pass — giving a spectacular view of the Dinwoody Creek Valley and Klondike, Pedestal, Flagstone, Bastion, Koven, Gannett and other Wind River Peaks — at 5.2 miles, and drops east to the Wind River Indian Reservation at mile 8.2. The Glacier Trail proceeds south then southwest up Dinwoody Creek Valley and passes these landmarks: Klondike Creek at mile 20.9, Wilson Meadows at mile 21.8, Gannett Creek(s) at mile 22.9 and the bottom of Dinwoody Glacier at mile 25.3. For technical climbing routes up Dinwoody Glacier past Gooseneck Pinnacle to Gannett Peak, check with the district ranger. See also *Wind River Trails* by Finis Mitchell and *Guide to the Wyoming Mountains and Wilderness Areas* by Orrin H. Bonney.

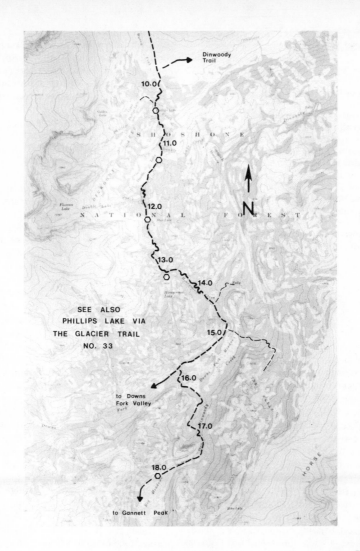

Dinwoody
Trail

10.0

11.0

12.0

13.0

14.0

15.0

SEE ALSO
PHILLIPS LAKE VIA
THE GLACIER TRAIL
NO. 33

16.0

to Downs
Fork Valley

17.0

18.0

to Gannett Peak

Double Lake

35 SLIDE LAKE

One day trip or backpack
Distances:
   Highline Trail - 2.6 miles/4.2KM.
   Clear Cr. Trail - 3.6 miles/5.8 KM.
   Slide Lake - 6.1 miles/9.8 KM.
Hiking time: 4-4½ hours one way
Elevation gain: 1,710 feet/216 M.
Elevation loss: 260 feet/79 M.
Maximum elevation : 9,500 feet/2,896 M.
Season: July through September
Topographic map:
   U.S.G.S. Green River Lakes, Wyo. 1968
Pinedale Ranger District
Bridger-Teton National Forest

The popular Green River Lakes Entrance to the Bridger Wilderness offers a variety of hiking and backpacking alternatives. For families, car campers, or those with limited time, the Lakeside Trail — a scenic, 6.1 mile loop around Lower Green River Lake with a view of famous Squaretop Mountain — provides an ideal one-day trip. This vista across the Green River Lakes past White Rock Range to Squaretop Mountain rates as one of the most beautiful in the United States and attracts hundreds of viewers each season, especially in July and August. This entrance serves also as a starting point for one- and two-week trips into the "Winds" via the Highline Trail to Summit Lake, another heavily over-used backpack corridor. Somewhat more secluded but still exceptionally scenic, Clear Lake, Slide Lake, or Twin, Shirley, and Valaite Lakes (No. 36) make good destinations for three-day trips. FISH: Wht, McKnw, Gryl in Lower Green River Lake; McKnw in Upper Green River Lake, Gdn in Clear Lake; Brk in Slide Lake.

Drive north on Wyo. 352 to the Green River Lakes Entrance, following the directions for the Twin, Shirley, and Valaite Hike (No. 36).

From the parking area hike south and east on the Highline/Lakeside access trail for 0.5 mile to the bridge below Green River Lake. Cross the bridge to a mileage sign reading "10 Three Fork Park/15 Summit Lake/24 New Fork Lake/30 Elkhart Park," etc. Fork right

onto the East Lakeside Trail and proceed on a delightfully rolling trek through sage and aspen around Green River Lake. At the start, a pointed, rock-topped mountain rises into view at 182°/SSW above the thick forested hillsides across the lake; near mid-lake two flat-topped summits beyond Upper Green River Lake join the exquisite skyline panorama at 150°/SSE. But the chief scenic glory throughout the lakeside walk is the sheer monolith of Squaretop Mountain south-southeast, sometimes mirrored in the blue lake waters, other times wrapped by fleecy clouds.

Pass willow-filled meadows beyond the upper end of the lake, come to a signed trail fork on a slight plateau in the trees at 2.6 miles, and turn left onto the Clear Creek Trail where the Highline Trail and West Lakeside Trail fork right to the valley floor. Switchback up a drainage to views of the massive, 11,823-foot Flat Top Mountain at 71°/E, soon joined on the right by the sheer, rugged White Rock Range and Squaretop Mountain. Cross a sage park at 2.7 miles where a sign indicates the noisy Clear Creek Falls, break into a large basin at mile 3.0 and follow treeline to a trail fork at 3.6 miles. (Here the Clear Creek Trail stays left, leads past Clear Creek Natural Bridge in another 1.1 miles, and reaches Clear Lake after 2.8 miles.) To proceed to Slide Lake, drop right across a bridge over Clear Creek — a point where the frothy-white Slide Creek Falls show at 124°/SE among dark conifers — and follow posts through the meadow to an unbridged crossing of Slide Creek after 3.9 miles.

Climb south through over a dozen switchbacks, passing beneath a thick, shady canopy of spruce and fir. Drop through a gully near 4.7 miles, traverse a slight plateau above Slide Creek where the view opens to the Green River Lakes at 272°/WNW, and enter another spacious basin at mile 4.9. After a zig-zag path southwest across the basin, re-enter conifers at 5.3 miles and make an easy climb to Fish Bowl Spring — a deep sandy pool filled with fingerling trout — at 5.6 miles. Begin a steeper climb along a slight ridge, passing views of the barren, rocky side of Flat Top Mountain at 17°/NNE, and cross a small saddle at 6.1 miles to the northwest side of Slide Lake. Skinny pine border the north side of the lake and extend toward the jagged, rocky range below Ram Pass. And across the lake at 118°/SE scree slopes and pinnacles shape part of Lost Eagle Peak.

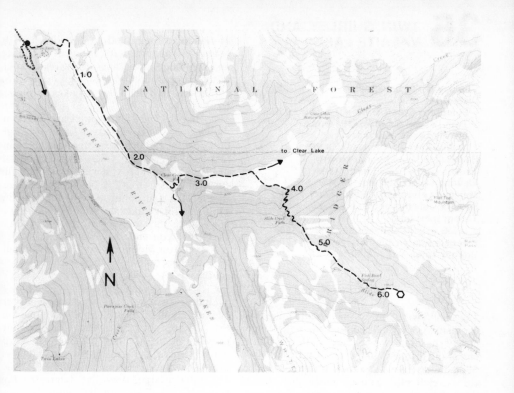

Squaretop Mountain beyond Green River Lake

36 TWIN, SHIRLEY, AND VALAITE LAKES

One day trip or backpack
Distances:
Porcupine Creek Trail - 4.3 miles/6.9 KM.
Twin Lakes - 6.3 miles/10.1 KM.
Shirley Lakes - 6.6 miles/10.6 KM.
Valaite Lake - 6.8 miles/10.9 KM.
Hiking time: 4½-5 hours one way
Elevation gain: 2,360 feet/719 M.
Elevation Loss: 320 feet/98 M.
Maximum elevation: 10,080 feet/3,072 M.
Season: July through September
Topographic map:
U.S.G.S. Green River Lakes, Wyo. 1968
Pinedale Ranger District
Bridger-Teton National Forest

The small Twin, Shirley, and Valaite Lakes fill exquisite, glacier-carved pockets in the range east of the Green River Lakes at the northern end of the Bridger Wilderness. Like Clear and Slide Lakes (No. 35), they provide a fairly close, relatively secluded destination for a three-day trip — one day in, one day fishing or exploring the Big Sheep Mountain Range above the lakes, and one day out. They also serve nicely as the first night's camp for a longer trip south to New Fork Park (No. 37) or Palmer Lake via the Porcupine Creek Trail, an excellent trip through sheltering and scenic valley bottoms off the beaten path of the Highline Trail. But perhaps the most appealing destination is timberline Lake Gadsby, reached with a map-and-compass trek south from Shirley Lake. FISH: Ct in Twin, Shirley, and Gadsby Lakes, none in Valaite.

Drive on U.S. 187 about 5.8 miles west of Pinedale to the junction with Wyo. 352, marked "Cora/Bridger Wilderness/Green River Entrance." Turn north, stay on the main road past the Cora turnoff at 4.3 miles, the Box R Ranch/WillowCreek Entrance at 8.1 miles, and the New Fork Lake Road at 14.8 miles, and proceed onto a dirt road after 19.4 miles. Continue past the Boulder Basin turnoff at 21.0 miles and the Whiskey Grove Campground at 28.8 miles, and come to the Green River Road/Union Pass Road fork after 29.3 miles, marked with a sign. Fork right and drive another 16.4 miles to the Green River Lakes parking area campground.

Follow the well-marked Highline/Lakeside access trail south from the parking area around the campground. Fork right where the Highline Trail turns left through a buck fence and continue to the Lakeside Trailhead south of the campground where a sign reads "Porcupine Creek Trail 3/Twin Lakes 7/Summit Lake 16/New Fork Lake 21/Elkhart Park 31." Hike through shady spruce and fir around the west side of Green River Lake, stay right past several campsites south of the lake, and fork right at 2.4 miles where an unsigned trail heads left (east) across a wide meadow. (This east trail crosses a bridge below Upper Green River Lake and connects with the Highline Trail and East Lakeside Trail.) In and out of view along this section are the rocky Clear Creek Canyon and the magnificent, 11,823-foot Flat Top Mountain east, and eventually the sheer, striated White Rock Cliffs east southeast.

Cross two branches of Porcupine Creek at 2.7 miles, curve right and begin a long, switchbacking climb up a forested hillside, reaching the ridgetop after 3.9 miles. Contour south through stands of pine for several hundred yards, swing right across a tributary, then recross the larger Porcupine Creek at 4.3 miles and enter a large, open flat. (Here the Porcupine Creek Trail forks left along treeline, climbs south for another 5.6 miles to Porcupine Pass, then drops to the New Fork Trail and Palmer Lake Trail.) Curve right (north) onto the Twin Lakes Trail, passing beautiful views of the unnamed, granite range next to Porcupine Creek. Soon begin another switchbacking climb west, cross Twin Lake Creek at 5.7 miles, and break out of scattered limber pine to an awe-inspiring panorama of northern Wind River Peaks. The alpine summits of Mount Solitude and Desolation Peak, usually covered with snow, can be seen at 102°/ESE. Gannett Peak marks the skyline farther south of that bearing; Rampart, Bastion, and Flagstone Peaks show to the north, all over 10½ miles away.

Contour southwest after this last climb to a scenic bowl at 6.2 miles which holds North Twin Lake. Wade the narrow neck of land between North and South Twin Lakes and climb steeply for 300 yards to the plateau containing scenic Shirley Lake, bordered on the south by green talus. Continue onto a trail at the northwest side of the lake, drafted onto the map, and climb west into the conifers, then contour for 250 more yards to the greenish gold waters of the upper Valaite Lake, encircled by unique, jagged rocks of yellows and golds.

Wild strawberry

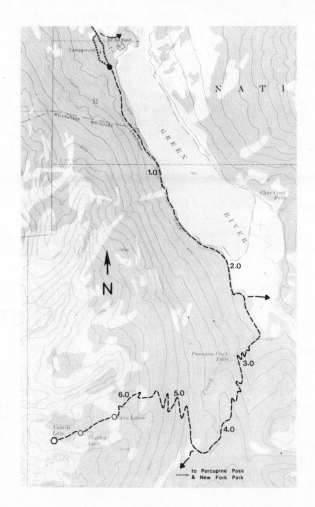

37 NEW FORK PARK

Backpack
Distances:
  Lowline Trail - 2.0 miles/3.2 KM.
  New Fork Trail - 7.0 miles/11.3 KM.
Hiking time: 4½ hours one way
Elevation gain: 1,410 feet/430 M.
Elevation loss: 550 feet/168 M.
Maximim elevation: 8,760 feet/2,670 M.
Season: July through early October
Topographic maps:
  U.S.G.S. New Fork Lakes, Wyo. 1967
  U.S.G.S. Kendall Mountain, Wyo, 1968
  U.S.G.S. Squaretop Mountain, Wyo. 1968
Pinedale Ranger District
Bridger-Teton National Forest

The New Fork Canyon Trail starts from The Narrows Campground on the north side of New Fork Lakes and thus makes a good route for car-camping families who want only a short sojourn into the Bridger Wilderness. Turnback points might be above the enchanting spruce-and-willow basin around the New Fork River at 2.5 miles or beneath the sheer granite walls and unique pillars in New Fork Canyon after 5.5 miles, a photographer's dream. On the splendid autumn day that the authors hiked the trail, they spent a quiet, half-hour watching a bull moose and his mate splash through the pools around the river and gambol in the meadows.

Drive on U.S. 187 about 5.8 miles west of Pinedale to the junction with Wyo. 352, marked "Cora/Bridger Wilderness/Green River Entrance." Turn north, pass the Cora turnoff at 4.3 miles and the Box R Ranch turnoff at 8.1 miles, and turn east onto the New Fork Lake Road at 14.8 miles, marked by a sign. Proceed past the Bridger National Forest boundary after another 2.5 miles, fork right to the "Narrows Campground" at 2.8 miles and park near the New Fork Canyon trailhead at the end of the campground loop, 5.0 miles from Wyo. 352.

Pass the trailhead sign which reads "8 New Fork Park," etc., head east over the clear path into rustling aspen groves, and soon cross two small brooks where drinking water can be obtained. Drop to the south side of the ridge at mile 0.7 where the upper New Fork Lake, lined with a dense wall of conifers, comes into view below and the rock-and-conifer side of New Fork Canyon, shadowed and creviced,

shows through the valley ahead at 35°/NE Continue the descent down the sage hillside to the upper end of the lake, swing right then left into the New Fork River Valley, and at 2. miles stay left past the signed Lowline Trail an alternate route to the Doubletop Mountain Trail and Rainbow Lake (No. 38). Pass the jumbled logs of an old log cabin (left), weave through pine clumps, then sage and aspen, and cross bridged drainageways after 2.6 miles Then continue the contour northeast along the valleyside above beautiful pools of water in the park (right) which cast shimmering reflections of silver-gray snags and tall pines.

Hop over a small creek near 3.7 miles, cross the Bridger Wilderness boundary in 20 more yards, then swing right on an easy climb through aspen and soon bend left to a good lookout of the New Fork River. Wind over the open rocky trail to views of high, granite pillars along the left side of New Fork Canyon, sheer wall farther right, and the long curve of the right canyonside beyond. Cross a main tributary near 4.3 miles, switchback left on a short climb, then enter the shade of a lodgepole pine forest and come to more drainages after 4.9 miles. Pass a rise (right) at 5. miles which blocks the view of the New Fork River, enter a narrower canyon and soon come to a river crossing among large boulders upstream from the horse crossing at 5.6 miles as shown on the U.S.G.S. topo. Cross here on fallen logs or wade the horse crossing downsteam; intercept the main trail south of the river and cross several tributaries on a contour at 61°/ENE up the basin. In close view now is the sheer, triangular rock wall which looms above the north side of the river surrounded by magnificent columns of stacked boulders.

Swing left (northeast) to another crossing over the New Fork River at 6.3 miles, switchback into scattered limber and lodgepole pine and wind north on a level grade into the southern reaches of New Fork Park. Pass the pillared east side of the Dome Peak Range (left and the rocky side of the unnamed, 10,985 foot mountain (right) and continue north through scattered spruce and pine, passing several campsites. The trail stays near treeline through the park and reaches a trail junction in another 1.2 miles just beyond a tributary creek. Here the Porcupine Creek Trail bears north toward Porcupine Pass and the Twin Lakes (No. 36) while the Palmer Lake Trail swings southeast into Palmer Canyon.

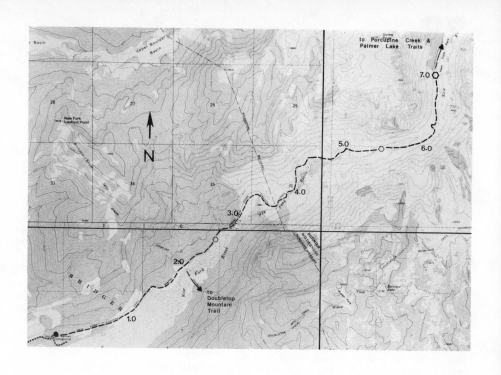

Inquisitive moose

38 RAINBOW LAKE

One day trip or backpack
Distances:
  Doubletop Mtn. Tr. - 2.2 miles/3.4 KM.
  Rainbow Lake - 4.4 miles/7.1 KM.
Hiking time: 3-3½ hours one way
Elevation gain: 2,320 feet/707 M.
Elevation loss: 40 feet/12 M.
Maximum elevation: 10,200 feet/3,109 M.
Season: July through early October
Topographic maps:
  U.S.G.S. New Fork Lakes, Wyo. 1967
  U.S.G.S. Fremont Lake North, Wyo. 1968
Pinedale Ranger District
Bridger-Teton National Forest

The less-developed Willow Creek Entrance usually attracts fewer of the tourists which plague the Elkhart Park, Big Sandy, and Green River Lake Entrances, but still provides quick access to many exquisite timberline lakes within the Bridger Wilderness. Besides Rainbow Lake, described below, there are Palmer and Penny Lakes in the Lake Creek Valley, the scores of Cutthroat and No Name Lakes via the Doubletop Mountain Trail, and the several Thompson and Hidden Lakes which lie north of Palmer Canyon beyond any constructed trails, all a backpacker's dream within range of a four-day trip. Summit Lake, heavily overused due to its crossroads location and thus **not** recommended as a campsite, lies farther east. It is passed by mountain climbers headed toward Mammoth Glacier, Mount Woodrow Wilson, and Gannett Peak. For mileages from Rainbow Lake, see the end of the text. FISH: Rbw and Brk in Rainbow Lake.

Drive on U.S. 187 about 5.8 miles west of Pinedale to the junction with Wyo. 352, marked "Cora/Bridger Wilderness/Green River Entrance." Turn north, proceed past the Cora turnoff at 4.3 miles, and turn right onto a gravel road just before 8.1 miles, marked privately as the Box R Ranch turnoff. Stay left past the Willow Creek Ranch turnoff after another 1.8 miles, stay left again past the Box R Ranch turnoff at 5.8 miles, then pass the Bridger National Forest boundary at 8.5 miles

and continue to the Willow Creek Guard Station, a total of 9.3 miles from Wyo. 230. Find off-the-road parking here or continue several hundred more yards, fork left across a Willow Creek tributary and park in the meadow beyond.

Follow the jeep trail north past a sign reading "Doubletop Mtn. Tr.," etc., cross a small sage opening and stay left toward the trailhead register and Willow Creek where the jeep road swings right. Cross the creek — filled with willows and beaver dams — at 0.3 mile, continue up the basin past willows, boggy tributaries, aspen and sage, then head north-northeast on a level trail through more aspen after 0.6 mile and make several short climbs crossing to the right of the tributary. Enter a cool forest of pine, spruce, whortleberry, and deadfall near 1.3 miles, bear north through two marshy parks after 1.8 miles where distant blue ranges come into view behind and are around an aspen grove (left) to the signed New Fork Lake/Rainbow Lake Trail junction at 2.2 miles.

Stay right as the Lowline Trail — an excellent early-season route, see No. 37 — climbs left (northwest) into the trees, bend gradually right (east) on a climb through dense pine after 2.4 miles, then make a final, short climb to a ridge at 2.7 miles and swing left into a rocky drainage. Head northeast across a slight plateau after 3.0 miles where the forested Willow Creek Valley can again be seen right. Wind near the creek on a steady climb up the rocky trail, break into an open basin after 3.4 miles as the trail levels, and bend right (east) into conifers on another climb. Enter grassy Martin Park near 3.9 miles which extends both right and left of the trail, and come to signs at the far end marking "Willow Cr. L.O. 1," etc. (The 10,232-foot Willow Creek Lookout lies due south through a saddle in 1 mile, no trail).

Cross and re-cross Willow Creek, then climb steadily along the left side to a slight ridge at 4.3 miles and soon break out onto a flat plateau near the cool, rippling waters of Rainbow Lake, the 4.4 mile mark. Large boulders and talus spill into the lake onto the far east side, a scenic hillside of conifers lines the south, and level, pine-needle campsites can be found beneath the twisted limber pine east of the lake. The Doubletop Mountain Trail passes north of the lake and then proceeds to other destinations: Palmer Lake — 3.2 miles, Cutthroat Lake — 5.0, West No Name Lake — 6.0, and Summit Lake — 8.2.

Early summer glissade

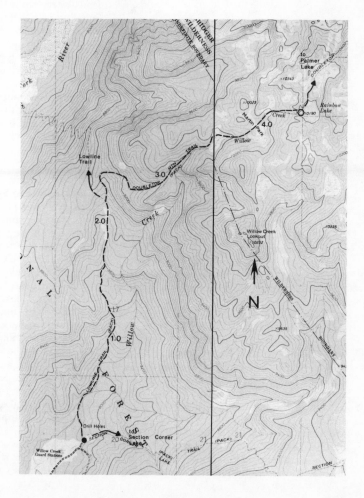

39 SECTION CORNER LAKE

Backpack
Distances:
  Indian Park - 2.2 miles/3.5 KM.
  Bluff Park Creek - 5.1 miles/8.2 KM.
  Section Corner Lake - 7.1 miles/11.4 KM.
Hiking time: 5-5½ hours one way
Elevation gain: 2,320 feet/707 M.
Elevation loss: 980 feet/299 M.
Maximum elevation: 9,540 feet/2,908 M.
Season: July through early October
Topographic maps:
  U.S.G.S. New Fork Lakes, Wyo. 1967
  U.S.G.S. Fremont Lake North, Wyo. 1968
Pinedale Ranger District
Bridger-Teton National Forest

Like the Doubletop Mtn. Trail to Rainbow Lake (No. 38) and beyond, the Section Corner Lake Trail begins at the relatively uncrowded Willow Creek Entrance and heads east into a wilderness paradise of high mountain lakes. Except for a brief glimpse near the Bridger Wilderness boundary at 3.3 miles, the jagged, alpine summits of the Wind River Range are not in view on this trip, a contrast to the spectacular vistas on the Pole Creek Trail to Seneca Lake (No. 41). The trail climbs and drops, winds in and out of tree clumps and crosses several creeks, creating a mood of seclusion and intimacy. Keep a sharp lookout for deer and bear. FISH: Brk, Brn and Gryl in Section Corner Lake.

Drive on Wyo. 352 and the Willow Creek Guard Station Road to the Willow Creek Entrance, following the driving instructions for Rainbow Lake (No. 38).

Follow a jeep trail east-northeast past the sign reading "Section Corner Lake Tr.," fork right after 60 yards at another sign, head east into a basin of willows (right), and come to the trail register near 0.1 mile. Continue over the single-path trail past a tumble-down log cabin and mounds of black soil (right), switchback left out of the basin at 0.8 mile and begin a steady, contouring climb up Big Flattop Mountain, crossing a drainage with sparkling, potable water at 1.2 miles. Break from the conifer cover across two small openings after 1.3 miles, then continue the climb through

loose switchbacks to the Big Flattop Mountain saddle at 2.1 miles, a good destination for a half-day's hike. Pass in and out of the northwestern tip of Indian Park — lush green grass in summer, sun-dried and yellow in fall — after 2.2 miles, curve right to a tree-enclosed park which slopes right at 2.6 miles, and at the far end pick up the well-worn Bluff Creek Trail, marked with a mileage sign.

Come to the Doubletop Mountain Trail cutoff just inside the trees at 2.7 miles, loop left around a ridge near 3.0 miles and drop gradually over the obvious trail through several hillside openings. Just beyond the Wilderness Boundary sign at 3.3 miles break out to a spectacular first vista of the rocky, alpine Wind River Peaks. At 49°/ENE the view extends through the saddle of American Legion Peak and Henderson Peak to 13,620-foot Mount Helen, and a jagged, serrated ridge leads north from this high point toward the equally-rugged Dinwoody and Doublet Peaks all over 12 miles away. In view also are the shining waters of Lily Pond Lake at 143°/SSE in the green basin below the trail. Bend right (south) along a tributary after 3.7 miles, follow the winding trail on several drops to a creek crossing at 4.2 miles, then swing left around a rocky wall to the open Bluff Park Creek Valley and eventually drop to a crossing of Bluff Creek near 5.1 miles (This creek leads north to Bluff Park in several more hundred yards, an excellent, off-the-beaten-path camping spot, see map).

To continue to Section Corner Lake, climb through limber pine to a higher hillside contour, soon fork right as directed by a sign and proceed to a drop across a tributary of Bluff Park Creek at 5.5 miles. Begin another climb east then south and eventually swing right across Lake Creek, marked by a sign at 5. miles. Wind east along the Lake Creek Valley crossing the creekbed four times over stone and fallen logs, and continue over the rolling trail to the west end of Section Corner Lake at 6.7 miles. The trail skirts the north side of the lake to a sandy beach at the Lake Creek inlet and connects at 7.1 miles in the willow basin north with the Round Lake/Palmer Lake Trail. Distances from this junction to other lakes: Round Lake — 2.5 miles, Palmer Lake — 3.8 miles, Trapper Lake via Section Corner Lake Trail — 1.2 miles, Trail Lake — 2. miles, Neil Lake — 3.0 miles, Gottfried Lake — 3.4 miles, Heart Lake — 3.6 miles, Borum Lake — 4.5 miles (see map).

Killdeer chick

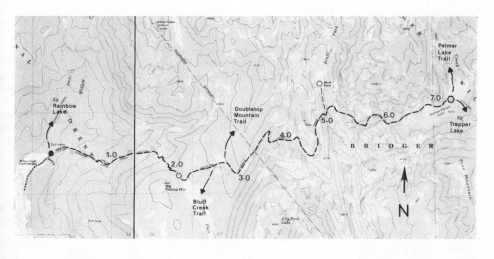

40 LONG LAKE

Backpack
Distance: 2.3 miles/3.7 KM. one way
Hiking time: 1½ hours one way
Elevation gain: 30 feet/9 M.
Elevation loss: 1,450 feet/442 M.
Maximum elevation: 9,330 feet/2,844 M.
Season: July through October
Topographic maps:
U.S.G.S. Fremont Lake North, Wyo. 1968
U.S.G.S. Bridger Lakes, Wyo. 1968
Pinedale Ranger District
Bridger-Teton National Forest

The short, steep drop to Long Lake makes the first leg of an adventurous, four- or five-day backpack trip up the Fremont Creek Valley. Similar to the steep-walled canyon around Ross Lake (No. 31), rugged, conifer-and-talus hillsides rise above Fremont Creek, Long Lake and Upper Long Lake, creating a barrier which keeps out all but the most persistent of backpackers. No trail is cut or maintained around the lakes — most of the valley lies within a designated Trailless Area — but sketchy use trails are worn around the south side of Long Lake, a route which eliminates a treacherous crossing of Fremont Creek. The best means of access into the valley, however, is with a backpackable rubber raft: 1.5 shoreline miles across Long Lake, a short, 0.2 mile climb-and-portage, then 0.8 miles across Upper Long Lake. FISH: Ct, Rbw, and Gryl in Long Lake; Rbw and Gryl in Upper Long Lake.

Like the Pole Creek Trail to Eklund Lake, etc. (No's. 41 & 42), the Pine Creek Canyon Trail to Long Lake suffers from heavy overuse, especially during July and August. Thus, this trail, although short, is not recommended as a half-day or one day hike; it serves best as access into the little-explored Fremont Creek Valley. Less traveled, more scenic half-day trips into the Bridger Wilderness are described in Slide Lake (No. 35) and Belford Lake (No. 44). Less traveled access to Trapper Lake is via the Section Corner Lake Trail (No. 39).

Drive on U.S. 187 to the east end of Pinedale

and proceed east onto the Fremont Lake Road, marked with a sign. Fork right after 3.3 miles onto the road to Halfmoon Lake and Elkhart Park, fork left at 7.3 miles where the right fork continues to Halfmoon Lake, then stay left at 10.4 miles past the turnoff to Fortification Mountain Ski Area. Follow the high road — now called Skyline Drive — above the northeast end of Fremont Lake. Pass the Elkhart Park Information Center and the south parking area, stay left past the campground turnoff, and park in the north parking area, a total of 15.3 miles from Pinedale.

From the parking area — the point of maximum elevation — a panorama of distant alpine Wind River Peaks can be seen above the nearby conifers, similar to the magnificent vistas from Skyline Drive and nearly the only distant view on the hike. 13,620-foot Mount Helen, 13,722-foot Mount Warren, Double and Dinwoody Peaks, 13,502-foot Mount Woodrow Wilson all stack up along the skyline near a 15°/NNE bearing. 13,804-foot Gannett Peak, highest point in Wyoming reaches its regal size at 5°/NNE, over 13 miles away. Pick up the Pine Creek Canyon Trail north of the parking area, marked by a sign listing "Trapper Lake 10/Summit Lake 15/New Fork Lake 29/Green River Lake 30," etc. Drop steadily on a well-used trail soon stop and fill out a card at the register box then continue the descent to a crossing over Faler Creek at 0.2 miles, a good opportunity for water fill-up.

Contour north as the Faler Creek drainage drops left and descend through a mixed forest of pine, spruce and fir. Soon bend northwest past openings which give glimpses of the high Wind River Range, and after 0.7 miles begin steeper drop through many short switchbacks. Swing west on the rocky trail past a jumble of boulders, marked "8875" on the topo, and come to a brief glimpse of the blue waters of Fremont Lake west. Drop steadily through more switchbacks, veering next to the deep ravine of Faler Creek; bend right after 1.1 miles through the only climbs of the trip and soon drop again along a forest floor of deadfall and pine needles. Continue north to the valley bottom, pass a sign marking the Bridger Wilderness boundary at 2.2 miles and come to the west edge of Long Lake in another 150 yards. Here the vista takes in the hillside of sparse pine and rock outcroppings north of Long Lake, and the steeper hillside of thick conifer and gray talus south.

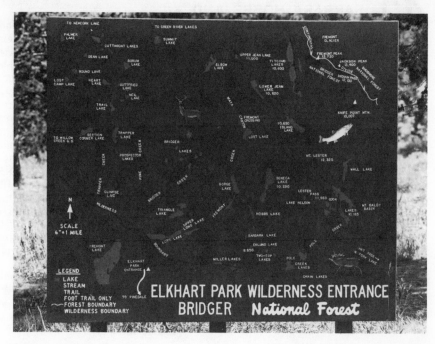

Elkhart Park entrance sign

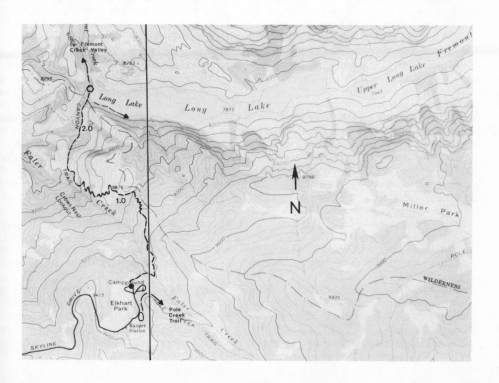

BARBARA, HOBBS, AND SENECA LAKES

Backpack
Distances:
  Eklund Lake - 5.6 miles/9.0 KM.
  Barbara Lake - 5.7 miles/9.2 KM.
  Hobbs Lake - 6.9 miles/11.1 KM.
  Seneca Lake - 8.9 miles/14.3 KM.
Hiking time: 5½-6 hours one way
Elevation gain: 1,710 feet/521 M.
Elevation Loss: 770 feet/235 M.
Maximum elevation: 10,370 feet/3,161 M.
Season: July through September
Topographic maps:
  U.S.G.S. Fremont Lake North, Wyo. 1968
  U.S.G.S. Bridger Lakes, Wyo. 1968
  U.S.G.S. Fayette Lake, Wyo. 1968
Pinedale Ranger District
Bridger-Teton National Forest

From the Elkhart Park Entrance — a rather citified departure point with an all-paved access, parking lots, campground and information center — the Pole Creek Trail begins a winding course east into the middle of the Wind River Range. The conspicuous absence of wild animals and the constant meeting with two-legged beasts in this part of the Bridger Wilderness detracts greatly from the trip, especially during the heavy backpacking months of July and August. The Entrance, in fact, receives more traffic than any other in the Bridger Wilderness, and the Pole Creek Trail shares more similarities with the tourist-lined pathways of a National Park than with a Wilderness. An undeniably spectacular vista of lofty Wind River Peaks, the all-weather access to the trailhead, and the relatively high — and hence energy saving — 9,300 foot start all contribute to the trail's popularity. But in spite of these advantages, the Pole Creek Trail, like the Pine Creek Canyon Trail to Long Lake (No. 40), can be recommended only for weeklong backpack trips in early July and in September. (See No. 42).

From Pinedale drive east on the Fremont Lake Road and on Skyline Drive to the **south** parking area in Elkhart Park, following the driving instructions for Long Lake (No. 40).

Begin hiking from the trailhead sign reading "Pole Creek Trail," etc. Make an easy climb southeast up the Faler Creek Valley, passing willow-filled meadows after 0.5 and 1.1 miles stay left past the Surveyor Park Trail turnoff a 1.4 miles and curve north on a delightful near-level contour through spruce and fir t the Bridger Wilderness boundary at 2.7 miles Enter a finger of Miller Park after 3.1 mile where distant peaks can be seen through th trees: Gannet Peak, the highest, towers int the skyline at 57°/ENE over 12 miles away an 13,745-foot Fremont Peak shows as th biggest block of stone at 14°/NNE. Continu through the main opening of Miller Park i several more yards, stay left on the Pole Cree Trail at 3.3 miles where the trail to Miller Lak — an alternate route, discussed in Cook Lak (No. 42) — forks right, then climb northeast i and out of conifers and loop around a smal tarn (right) at 4.5 miles. Here a magnificen panorama of canyons, lakes, glaciers, and al pine peaks opens from 322°/NNW to 38°/NE making this point — or the equally-sceni Photographers Point north — a superb one day destination.

Stay left where the Miller/Sweeney Lake Trail rejoins from the right (south) at 5.2 mile and continue into the trees to the Pole Cree Trail and Seneca Lake Trail tri-junction a mile 5.5, marked with mileage signs. Fork le away from Eklund Lake, in view southeast Drop gradually to the west side of Barbar Lake at mile 5.7 where the view again extend to skyline spires at 348°/N. Cross the outle creek west of the lake, bear northwest along rock wall with a drainage left, and soon dro through switchbacks to a grassy valley bottor at 6.3 miles. Pass a small pond (right), clim steadily northeast past rock outcroppings an limber pine clumps, and break out on the wes side of Hobbs Lake — surrounded by a mor austere landscape of wind-twisted conifer and gray rock — at 6.9 miles. Cross two bridged outlet creeks north of the lake, ste stones over two more tributaries in a ver scenic section of white and gray, angula boulders and splashing cascades, and pas ponds at miles 7.6 and 7.8 on a steady switch backing drop. Bend right (east-northeast above a grassy pond at 8.1 miles and make final switchbacking climb past glacial-pol ished boulders to a viewpoint at 8.8 miles o mile-long Seneca Lake. The round, rock mound of Lester Mountain rises beyond th lake at 51°/ENE, and the massive Continenta Divide range near Mt. Helen shows a 359°/NNE.

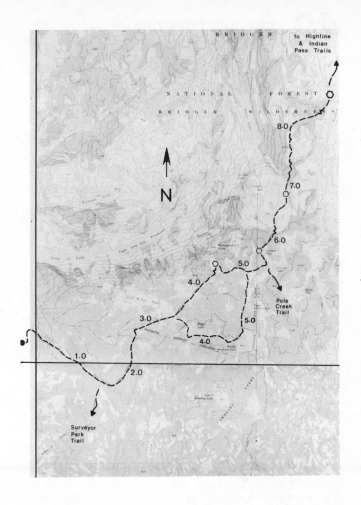

Vista near the start

99

42 EKLUND, POLE CREEK, AND COOK LAKES

Backpack
Distances: Miller Lake - 3.7 miles/6.0 KM.
 Eklund Lake - 6.2 miles/10.0 KM.
 Pole Creek Lake - 9.7 miles/15.6 KM.
 Cook Lake - 13.0 miles/20.9 KM.
Hiking time: 7-8 hours one way
Elevation gain: 2,340 feet/713 M.
Elevation loss: 1,500 feet/457 M.
Maximum elevation: 10,330 feet/3,149 M.
Season: July through September
Topographic maps:
 U.S.G.S. Fremont Lake North, Wyo. 1968
 U.S.G.S. Bridger Lakes, Wyo. 1968
 U.S.G.S. Fayette Lake, Wyo. 1968
 U.S.G.S. Fremont Peak South, Wyo. 1968
Pinedale Ranger District
Bridger-Teton National Forest

After the usual "Labor Day snowstorm" in the Wind River Range which quickly routs the summer hikers and marks a final end to any remaining mosquitoes, the Wilderness becomes an enchanting paradise for peaceful, week-long backpacking odysseys. Autumn colors decorate every vista: The aspen turn brilliant hues of yellow and gold and tawny grass blankets each meadow. Splashes of russet from geranium, creeping barbelly, and sulphurflower appear along the rocky hillsides. From early September on, the Pole Creek Trail from the Elkhart Park Entrance can be hiked in reasonable solitude. It makes the first leg of a thrilling trip toward timberline Seneca, Island, and Titcomb Lakes as well as the Alpine Lakes via Indian Pass east of the Continental Divide (see No. 41). Or it can be followed to Cook and Wall Lakes or the less-visited Chain, Spruce, and Junction Lakes loop.

From Pinedale drive east on the Fremont Lake Road and on Skyline Drive to the **south** parking area in Elkhart Park, following the driving instructions for Long Lake (No. 40).

Pick up the Pole Creek Trail at the northeast end of the parking area, climb gradually southeast up Faler Creek Valley, and swing north to the Miller Lake turnoff at 3.3 miles, as described in the Barbara Lake hike (No. 41). To loop past Miller, Middle Sweeney, and Upper Sweeney Lakes, angle right where the Pole Creek Trail forks left (northeast). Drop quickly to the west side of Miller Lake at mile 3.7, loop east past the lake (left), then pass a

small pond (left) at 4.5 miles, and swing left by old cabin ruins where a right fork contours to Middle Sweeney Lake. Climb up an open hillside above willows (right), and soon gain a vantage of distant Wind River Peaks ahead. At 352°/N majestic Gannett Peak appears highest in the skyline, flanked left by Bow Mountain, Mount Arrowhead, and American Legion Peak and right by Mount Woodrow Wilson. Pointed Mt. Helen, blanketed on the right by Fremont Glacier, shows at 1°/NNE, and soon the familiar hump of Fremont Peak soars into the horizon line at 8°/NNE.

Skirt a pond (right), rejoin the rutted Pole Creek Trail at 5.8 miles, and continue northeast into conifers to the well-marked Pole Creek Trail and Seneca Lake Trail tri-junction at 6.1 miles. Bear right (southeast) to Eklund Lake at mile 6.2; drop down switchbacks and wind east past unnamed ponds left then right and break to a view of Marys Lake — with several wide channels, enclosed by rock and trees — at 7.0 miles. Drop east through more switchbacks after 7.3 miles, follow an open drainage to long and narrow Mosquito Lake (left) at mile 7.8, then proceed east past the No Name Lake turnoff at 8.2 miles and wind past scenic ponds to the Monument Creek crossing at 9.1 miles. Drop southeast along a drainage (right) to a tributary crossing at 9.7 miles, climb and drop over a knoll north of Pole Creek Lake and come to a junction with the Highline Trail east of another Pole Creek Lake, the 9.9 mile mark.

To proceed to the Cook Lakes, follow the Highline Trail to a crossing of Pole Creek at 10.1 miles above the north side of the Pole Creek Lake. Continue east and northeast by creek loops and tarns, climb and drop across a rocky knoll after mile 10.7, then pass twin ponds and a main tributary and come to the Fremont Trail junction (possibly unmarked) at 11.4 miles. In a few more yards make a second crossing of Pole Creek, swing north to the crossing of a Pole Creek tributary at mile 11.6 and stay on the left side to an obscure tri-junction at mile 11.9. Here the Highline Trail turns left (northwest) on a climb to Cook Lake "10175", Tommy Lake, Lake Nelson and Lester Pass. The middle fork bears north-northeast to the large Cook Lakes "10143" and "10170", while another branch of the Fremont Trail, more clearly seen across the tributary, turns right around the east side of Mount Baldy, in view at 140°/SSE.

Wildflower relief

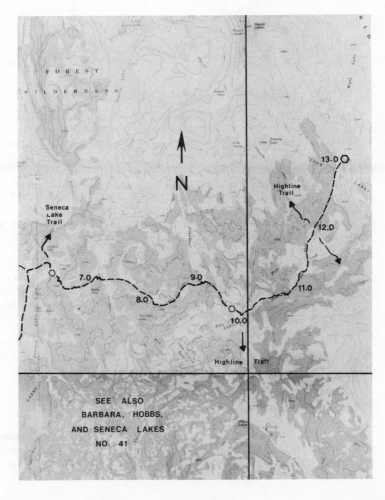

43 FAYETTE LAKE

One day trip
Distance: 3.3 miles/5.3 KM. one way
Hiking time: 2-2½ hours one way
Elevation gain: 1,110 feet/338 M.
Elevation loss: 770 feet/235 M.
Maximum elevation: 8,200 feet/2,499 M.
Season: Late June through mid-October
Topographic map:
  U.S.G.S. Fayette Lake, Wyo. 1968
Pinedale Ranger District
Bridger-Teton National Forest

A good choice for families and young hikers, this trail climbs the slight knoll behind Upper Half Moon Campground, makes a wet crossing of Pole Creek northeast of Half Moon Lake, and contours east among sage knolls to Fayette Lake. The recently-constructed route is not marked on the 1968 U.S.G.S. Fayette Lake topo but has been drafted onto the map photo. It stays west of the Bridger Wilderness within the Bridger National Forest, winding through little-visited lowlands which offer a good possibility for seeing elk or mule deer. For a nearby route into the Bridger Wilderness itself, see Belford Lake (No. 44).

Drive on U.S. 187 to the east end of Pinedale and proceed east onto the Fremont Lake Road, marked with a sign. Turn right after 3.3 miles where a sign reads "Halfmoon Lake," then turn right again at 7.3 miles where the left fork continues to Elkhart Park. Proceed on this gravel road for another 2.6 miles along the north side of Half Moon Lake to Upper Half Moon Campground and park in the small turn-around area.

Descend to Half Moon Campground and climb southeast past the tables and outhouse to a slight saddle at mile 0.1. Take the main trail east-southeast, soon pass through a buck

fence, and drop into pine, aspen and sage toward the north shore of Half Moon Lake. Cross a grove of aspen and cedar after 0.4 mile where the "toe" of Half Moon Lake can be seen at 134°/SSE. Continue the rolling contour east and northeast above the lakeshore, swing left on a gradual climb at mile 0.9, then dip through a grassy drainage at mile 1.2 and soon swing south past an old "Pole Creek/Lowline Trail" sign to the "heel" of the lake, a possible picnic spot and turn-back point.

To proceed to Fayette Lake, wade the knee-deep water at this 1.4 mile mark, make a slight climb along a gully, and fork left (east) onto the Fayette Lake Trail where the Half Moon Trail turns right (south). Drop over a ridge to the Pole Creek Valley at 1.7 miles, climb to a tributary crossing at 2.0 miles, then climb past two protruding ridges at miles 2.2 and 2.6 and come to a good view of the south end of Fayette Lake. Take a southerly bearing to a slight drainage at 3.0 miles, swing east across a small tributary at mile 3.1, and in a few more yards join the Half Moon Trail Cutoff. End the hike with a short drop north to Fayette Lake.

Cold water swimmer

44 BELFORD LAKE

One day trip or backpack
Distances:
   Timico Lake Trail - 3.7 miles/6.0 KM.
   Belford Lake - 5.9 miles/9.5 KM.
Hiking time: 4½-5 hours one way
Elevation gain: 2,300 feet/701 M.
Elevation loss: 360 feet/110 M.
Maximum elevation: 9,640 feet/2,938 M.
Season: July through early October
Topographic map:
   U.S.G.S. Fayette Lake, Wyo. 1968
Pinedale Ranger District
Bridger-Teton National Forest

Undeveloped and unpublicized, the Little Half Moon Lake Entrance is sandwiched between the more elaborate—and hence much busier—Elkhart Park Entrance north and Boulder Lake Entrance south. The gravel access road can be rutted and slow after rains, and the Little Half Moon Campground is nothing more than a picnic table or two. But a hike into the Bridger Wilderness from this starting point offers quiet solitude, a good chance of seeing mule deer on the sage hillsides, plus quick access to many mid-Wilderness lakes. The Timico Lake to North Fork Canyon to Hay Pass route is shorter than the one from the Boulder Lake Entrance via North Fork Lake (see No. 46). Climb the first hillside to mile 1.5 or so for a splendid half-day trip; pack drinking water on the hike to Belford Lake; take time for a sidetrip from the Timico Lake Trail to beautiful-but-often-bypassed Lake Sequa. FISH: Brk in Belford Lake.

From the junction with the Fremont Lake Road at the east end of Pinedale, drive on U.S. 187 another 0.9 mile south to an unsigned gravel road. Turn left (east), turn left again after another 4.5 miles where the Fall Creek Ranch Road bends right, then turn left at 5.5 miles and stay right at 7.1 miles. Climb north along a ridgetop, wind south then north for almost two miles, and make a final, short descent southeast to the south end of Little Half Moon Lake, 11.2 miles from U.S. 187.

Bend right from the Little Half Moon Campground to a wet crossing of Pole Creek. Swing right (east) from the southeast side of the lake, pass through an aspen grove and fork left at 21°/NE from the middle of the second grove to the main trail. Climb steadily along a draw (left) after 0.5 mile, soon traverse across the draw to a good viewpoint of Little Half-moon Lake, and continue the climb through more winds to a trail junction at 1.3 miles. Stay left where the right fork leads toward Meadow and Burnt Lakes, crest to the top of the sage rise in 25 more yards, and begin climbing north up the ridge. Here far-away ranges come into view: At 224°/WSW and continuing left, flat, distant-blue Commissary Ridge (No. 1) spreads across the skyline. High, indistinct mountains near Hoback Peak in the Wyoming Range show at 270°/WNW, and others, more rugged, rise at 300°/NW near Pyramid Peak in the Gros Ventre Range. But the most engaging panorama is of glistening Half Moon and Little Half Moon Lakes, nestled within aspen and sage hills.

Climb gradually north-northeast around a sage basin (right), turn left at the draw at 2.1 miles, and make a steep, switchbacking climb to the ridgetop. At this point Meadow Lake at 162°/S and Burnt Lake at 133°/SSE return to view while the magnificent Cirque of the Towers near Lizard Head Peak makes a brief appearance on the skyline at 96°/ESE. Cross another draw at 2.3 miles, loop around a park (left) at mile 2.6, then make a winding climb to a ridgetop course at mile 3.3 and bear east through sage above an aspen hillside (right) to the Timico Lake Trail at 3.7 miles. Enter pine on a switchbacking climb northeast, pass marshes (left) at 4.0 miles, then cross the Bridger Wilderness boundary near mile 4.6 and contour above a south-facing hillside to a slight descent at 5.0 miles. Climb gradually into an open flat at mile 5.3 where sheer, serrated Wind River Peaks flash through the tree openings. Rugged Mt. Lander appears highest in the middle of the vista at 86°/ESE, and farther up the trail, pointed peaks — possibly East Temple Peak at 105°/ESE and the Cirque of the Towers to the left — come into view. Continue to the south end of Belford Lake at mile 5.9 where the ruins of Black's Cabin — six logs high, ten feet square, with a stone fireplace — can be seen. A few yards beyond, the Timico Lake Trail forks right (northeast) toward Jacquline and Barnes Lakes and the Highline Trail.

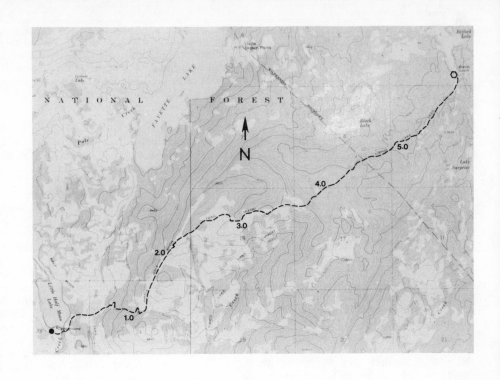

Discards

Black's cabin at Belford Lake

45 COYOTE LAKE

One day trip or backpack
Distance: 5.9 miles/9.5 KM. one way
Hiking time: 4½-5 hours one way
Elevation gain: 2,495 feet/760 M.
Elevation loss: 255 feet/78 M.
Maximum elevation: 9,540 feet/2,908 M.
Season: July through early October
Topographic maps:
    U.S.G.S. Scab Creek, Wyo. 1968
    U.S.G.S. Boulder Lake, Wyo. 1964
    U.S.G.S. Fayette Lake, Wyo. 1968
    U.S.G.S. Horseshoe Lake, Wyo. 1968
Pinedale Ranger District
Bridger-Teton National Forest

Four exciting trails branch out from Coyote Lake, making it a logical destination for a base camp. The North Fork Trail, described below as the route to the lake but also an excellent route for a return loop, bears west. It crosses the many marshes and tributaries above Blueberry Lake (prime mule deer and moose habitat) and then loops past the Burnt Lake/Lowline Trail to Boulder Lake Campground. The Blueberry Trail, a complement route for either the entry or return, drops south from Coyote Lake and connects Cross, Lovatt (with a side link), and Blueberry (Ruff on the Forest Service map) Lakes. The Horseshoe Lake Trail, now unmaintained by the Forest Service, holds a northerly bearing from Coyote Lake to large Horseshoe Lake where it joins with the Highline Trail. And from a junction north of Coyote Lake, the North Fork Trail proceeds east to George, Edmund (different than Eds), Macs, and North Fork Lakes. Rather than camp near the lakes, use the U.S.G.S. topo or the map photo on the opposite page to find a secluded site along the many tributaries. FISH: Brk in Lovatt and Blueberry Lakes; Brk and Gdn in Cross Lake.

Drive on U.S. 187 to Boulder, 12.0 miles southeast of Pinedale. Turn east onto Wyo. 353 and proceed another 2.5 miles to the signed junction with the Boulder Lake Road (Sublette Co. 23-125). Turn left (north), stay right after another 5.0 miles where a road to Stokes Crossing forks left, and continue east above the south side of Boulder Lake to a locator map at 10.5 miles. As this map indicates, a parking and backpack assembly area

has been constructed left of the road in another 0.1 mile. The Boulder Creek Canyon and Ruff Lake Trail begin on the right in 0.2 miles and the Boulder Lake Campground, with another trailhead for Ruff and Coyote Lakes, lies across Boulder Creek.

Intercept the signed "Trail" north of the campground loop; cross through a buck fence to the North Fork Trail and proceed north-northwest through a beautiful grove of aspen. Swing left across a tributary at mile 0.2, begin a rolling climb left of the tributary where the view soon encompasses much of glistening Boulder Lake and the surrounding hills, and come to the junction of the Blueberry and North Fork Trails at 0.7 mile. To take the North Fork Trail to Coyote Lake, fork left, enter more aspen on a curve right, and continue on a steep, winding climb to another lookout of Boulder Lake. At 68°/E the slightest tips of peaks around Mt. Lander mark the horizon. Pass through a draw at mile 1.0 to another steep climb up the sage hillside. Stay right at 1.8 miles on the North Fork Trail where the Lowline Trail forks left, follow posts through a sage corridor and funnel into skinny pine and across a narrow glen. As the hillside begins to rise, turn right at 58°/ENE and maintain a climb, reaching the Bridger Wilderness sign near 2.9 miles.

Cross a tributary in 20 more yards, swing right over a slight rise which marks the actual Wilderness boundary and drop through a draw where a use trail joins right. Proceed north-northwest from a ridgetop (where Blueberry Lake comes into view) to the forest floor to a hillside contour. Cross a draw at mile 3.8, climb then drop to a crossing of Blueberry Creek, then loop around a park (left) and re-cross the creek at mile 4.0. Climb steeply northwest then north to a swampy flat (right), swing right after 4.6 miles on a winding course through rocks and conifers, and continue up another drainage where a use trail crosses from right to left. Pass a tiny pond (left) at mile 5.0, cross a swampy park which opens right, then continue through rocky, open terrain past another pond (right) at mile 5.4 and curve right past a park (left) to a tributary crossing at mile 5.6. Bear west-northwest along another drainage to the west side of Coyote Lake, the 5.9 mile mark. From a junction north of the lake, the Horseshoe Lake Trail splits north while the North Fork Trail continues east.

To make a return loop past Cross, Lovatt,

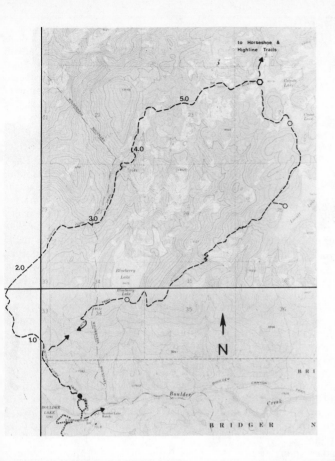

Sticky geranium

and Blueberry Lakes, wind south along Coyote Lake to the outlet crossing at the southwest end. Loop around a pond (right) and pass Cross Lake (left), then follow the basin past another pond (left) and eventually break from conifers to a viewpoint of Lovatt Lake south (see map). A panoramic vista of Wind River Peaks spread across the horizon beyond: At 80°/E the 12,570-foot-high mound of Mt. Bonneville; at 93°/ESE the rounded, alpine summit of Mt. Washakie; at 99°/ESE the pointed spires of the famous Cirque of the Towers, the most impressive part; and at 107°/ESE the tilted knob of 12,976-foot Temple Peak. Proceed southwest on a rolling, ridgeline descent for over a mile, drop south through pine and sage and make a zig-zag drop to Blueberry Lake. Cross the outlet and continue the winding descent down the north valleyside of Boulder Creek to Boulder Lake Campground, a 6.5 mile trip from Coyote Lake.

46
ETHEL, CHRIS, MACS, AND NORTH FORK LAKES

Backpack
Distances:
  Lake Ethel - 6.2 miles/10.0 KM.
  Lake Christina - 8.5 miles/13.7 KM.
  Macs Lake - 10.3 miles/16.6 KM.
  North Fork Lake - 12.4 miles/20.0 KM.
Hiking time: 7-8 hours one way
Elevation gain: 2,850 feet/869 M.
Elevation loss: 390 feet/119 M.
Maximum elevation: 9,850 feet/3,002 M.
Season: July through September
Topographic maps:
  U.S.G.S. Scab Creek, Wyo. 1968
  U.S.G.S. Horseshoe Lake, Wyo. 1968
Pinedale Ranger District
Bridger-Teton National Forest

The well-traveled Boulder Canyon Trail begins at the Boulder Lake Entrance and heads east into the Bridger Wilderness along Boulder Creek beneath high, beautiful canyon walls. With a turnoff at Lake Ethel at 5.8 miles, routes can be linked north and northeast to dozens of sub-alpine lakes, all of any size with good fishing. For a superb, ten-day trip, cross the Continental Divide via North Fork Canyon and Hay Pass and explore the alpine lakes in the Shoshone National Forest, blocked from the east by the Wind River Indian Reservation.

Drive to the Boulder Lake Entrance at the middle of the Bridger Wilderness, following directions for Coyote Lake (No. 45.)

Begin from the trailhead sign reading "Boulder Cr. Canyon" south of Boulder Creek. Pass through a buck fence, bear east into aspen groves past the Boulder Lake Ranch (right) at 0.2 mile, and stay on the Boulder Canyon Trail past the North Fork Trail Cutoff at a bridge. Follow the road across a sage flat and into aspen, continue onto a one-lane trail at the register near 0.7 mile, and cross to the north side of Boulder Creek afte 1.1 miles. Break from lush aspen and conifers onto a sage knoll, climb gradually to tributary crossings at 1.7 and 1.8 miles, then swing left (east) along a marshy drainage and rejoin the Boulder Creek Valley at 2.6 miles. Soon funnel into a narrower — and exceptionally scenic — canyon: cross tributaries at 2.7, 3.4 (Macs Creek), 4.3, and 4.9 miles and pass

above green pools of water — filled with darting trout — in Boulder Creek. Bend north, climb through switchbacks with many good viewpoints of the rocky, conifer-laced canyon, and come to a junction of the Boulder Canyon Trail (see No. 47) and Lake Ethel Trail at mile 5.8.

Fork left, climb steadily north past the North Fork Falls and through a fire-burned area, and soon begin an easy descent to Lake Ethel at 6.2 miles. Continue the switchbacking climb north-northwest up the valley, break out to tree-ringed Eds Lake at 7.3 miles, soon pass an interesting beaver lodge and beaver-cut channels at the lake's upper end, then stay left past the signed turnoff to the Norman Lakes at mile 7.5. Re-cross the creek, make another switchbacking climb to large Lake Christina at 8.5 miles, then skirt left of the lake and bear northeast along Macs Creek to Perry Lake — enclosed in a small rock-and-aspen basin — at mile 9.7. Climb northeast again along a conifer-cluttered drainage, recross Macs Creek and contour to the south end of Macs Lake at 10.3 miles. Cross the lily-pad-covered inlet to a junction with the Highline Trail at mile 10.6, the main Bridger Wilderness route which bears north-northwest to Lakes Edmund, George, and Horseshoe (see Coyote Lake No. 45), then to Barnes, Chain, and Pole Creek Lakes (see Belford Lake and Pole Creek Lake No's. 44 and 42), then to Seneca Lake (see No. 41), and finally to the Green River Lakes (see No's. 35 and 36).

Fork right (northeast), wind past slow-moving ponds left at mile 10.8, then right at mile 11.2, and come to a slight saddle at mile 11.6. Loop left around an open flat, pass the Highline Trail Cutoff at 11.8 miles, then continue past the pond (right) and enter a grassy basin. Here the gray, massive Wind River Peaks come into view on the skyline: At 330°/NNW a rocky knob protrudes to the right of Hat Pass, the Fremont Trail route to Cook Lakes (No. 42). Farther right at 342°/N is more rounded North Fork Peak which lies left of the North Fork Canyon and Hay Pass Trail. Highest, with scree slopes and rock walls, Mt. Victor comes to a point at 15°/NNE, framed by more distant peaks behind. Continue northwest away from a green-roofed log cabin across the basin to reach island-studded North Fork Lake. To get to Winona and Vera Lake (No. 47), cross the southeast neck of North Fork Lake near an old campsite and bear south on the Highline Trail.

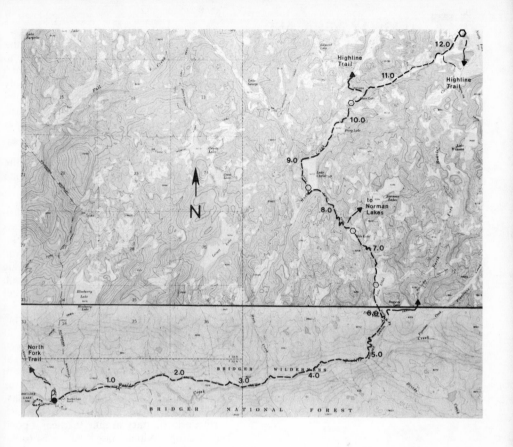

Woods walk

North Fork Lake

47 DUGWAY, VERA, AND WINONA LAKES

Backpack
Distances:
  Dugway Lake - 6.3 miles/10.1 KM.
  Vera Lake - 9.5 miles/15.3 KM.
  Winona Lake - 10.4 miles/16.7 KM.
Hiking time: 6-7 hours one way
Elevation gain: 2,825 feet/861 M.
Elevation loss: 435 feet/133 M.
Maximum elevation: 9,860 feet/3,005 M.
Season: July through September
Topographic maps:
  U.S.G.S. Scab Creek, Wyo. 1968
  U.S.G.S. Horseshoe Lake, Wyo. 1968
  U.S.G.S. Mt. Bonneville, Wyo. 1938*
  *15 minute series
Pinedale Ranger District
Bridger-Teton National Forest

While the hike to Ethel, Chris, Macs, and North Fork Lakes (No. 46) from the Boulder Lake Entrance describes a northern entry into the middle of the Bridger Wilderness, this hike, as far as Lake Vera at 9.5 miles, charts a more southern one. After a first night's camp at Lake Vera, the trip can be continued to dozens of other prime-fishing lakes along the Highland Trail corridor and to lakes farther west within the alpine Wind River Peaks (see below). Three- and four-day loop trips are more easily arranged from this Entrance than from any other, due to the numerous cross trails. Here are a few examples, with smaller trips first: Ethel Lake to Macs Lake to Coyote Lake to Ruff Lake (see No's. 45 and 46). Or Lake Vera to Lake Winona to North Fork Lake to Lake Ethel, which combines No's. 46 and 47. Or Lake Vera to Fire Hole Lakes to Howard Lake to North Fork Lake, which expands the loop between No's. 46 and 47. Plan these trips from the Boulder Lake Entrance for September (and with provisions for cold weather, for early October). Consider the less-crowded Little Half Moon Entrance to Belford Lake (No. 44) and Scab Creek Entrance to Little Divide Lake (No. 48) during July and August. Expect some horse travel on the Boulder Canyon Trail. FISH: Brk in Ethel, Ed's, Chris, and Perry Lakes; Ct in Vera, Winona, and North Fork Lakes.

Drive to the Boulder Lake Entrance at the middle of the Bridger Wilderness, following directions for Coyote Lake (No. 45).

Hike east on the Boulder Canyon Trail to the Lake Ethel Trail turnoff at mile 5.8, as described in the North Fork Lake hike (No. 46). Stay right where the Lake Ethel Trail climbs left, cross the bridge over the cascading North Fork Creek, then climb through switchbacks away from Boulder Canyon and swing east to the bottom end of Dugway Lake at 6.3 miles. Enter thick fir on a switchbacking climb to a slight saddle northeast of the lake at mile 6.9, follow a narrow passage between high boulders, and pass a small pond (left) at mile 7.4. Make another switchbacking climb southeast, swing left (northeast) above the steep Pipestone Creek Valley after 8.0 miles, and contour over slight ridges to a crossing of a North Fork tributary at mile 9.2 near a pond (right). Drop gradually north-northeast to the south end of Lake Vera at 9.5 miles where trails split right and left.

To get to Jonkey, Fire Hole, Full Moon, Junction, and eventually Raid and South Fork Lakes, fork right (east). This vast and beautiful region, also reached via the Scab Creek Trail from Little Divide Lake (No. 48) has cross routes which link with the main Highline Trail and which proceed to high alpine lakes. Junction Lake to Halls or Middle Fork Lakes via the Middle Fork Boulder Creek, and Dream Lake to Rainbow, Sunrise, and the Bonneville Lakes are exciting routes for week-long backpack trips. To get from Lake Vera to Lake Winona (as figured for the information capsule), take the left (north) fork. Climb past jumbled talus and boulders north of Lake Vera and cross a bridge beneath a pond (right) at 9.9 miles. Then skirt a marshy park (left) and a tiny pond (right) at 10.2 miles and drop northwest through a drainage to the southeast end of Lake Winona at mile 10.4. From this point the trail proceeds north to North Fork Lake (see No. 46), another 1.3 miles.

Chipmunk sentinel

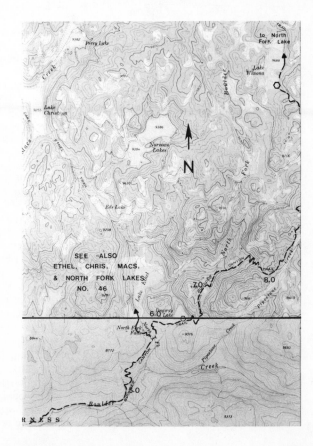

SEE ALSO
ETHEL, CHRIS, MACS,
& NORTH FORK LAKES
NO. 46

48 TOBOGGAN, LITTLE DIVIDE, AND DIVIDE LAKES

One day trip or backpack
Distances:
   Toboggan Lake - 4.0 miles/6.4 KM.
   Little Divide Lake - 5.6 miles/9.0 KM.
   (Divide Lake - 6.2 miles/10.0 KM.)
Hiking time: 3½-4 hours one way
Elevation gain: 1,780 feet/543 M.
Elevation loss: 380 feet/116 M.
Maximum elevation: 9,680 feet/2,950 M.
Season: Late June through mid-October
Topographic maps:
   U.S.G.S. Scab Creek, Wyo. 1968
   U.S.G.S. Mt. Bonneville, Wyo. 1938*
   *15 minute series
Pinedale Ranger District
Bridger-Teton National Forest

The Lowline Trail from the Scab Creek Entrance begins with an uninspiring trek across dry sage hills and past marshy ponds, a public access through private property which lacks the grand vistas of, say, the Green River Lakes or Elkhart Park Entrances. But fortunately this route also lacks the constant stream of backpackers. And despite its unextraordinary beginning, it provides the quickest way into the middle third of the Bridger Wilderness. Dozens of prime fishing lakes cover this area, many little-visited throughout the summer, and from the spacious South Boulder Creek basin, the towering Wind River Peaks finally appear in a magnificent panorama. Famed "Man O' the Mountains" Finis Mitchell, in his guidebook *Wind River Trails,* sums up his feelings about this part of the Wilderness with these words: "In my opinion, neither Dictator nor King has a more divine land elsewhere on the globe." FISH: Brk in Toboggan and Divide Lakes; Brk, Rbw in Little Divide Lake.

The Lowline Trail connects with the Scab Creek Trail near Little Divide Lake, the point figured for the information capsule. For a delightful five-day trip in the montane zone, either continue south via the Lowline Trail to Divide, Monroe, Star, and Wolf Lakes or bear east via the Scab Creek Trail to South Fork and Raid Lakes, then south to Cross, Upper Silver, and Silver Lakes. To the northeast in the high alpine country are beautiful Halls, Middle Fork and Bonneville Lakes, worthy destinations for longer trips. Backpack here in July and August; take the U.S.G.S. Mt. Bonneville topo; purify drinking water against possible contamination.

From Pinedale drive southeast on U.S. 187 for 12 miles to the junction with Wyo. 353 at Boulder. Turn east, proceed past the Boulder Lake turnoff after 2.5 miles and come to the signed Scab Creek Access just beyond green government buildings, 6.7 miles from U.S. 187. Turn left (northeast), turn left again after 1.5 miles, and continue another 7.2 miles to the Lowline Trailhead parking area. The Lowline Trail junction is another 0.1 mile down the road, the Scab Creek Campground another 0.4 mile.

Pick up the trail near the sign reading "Lowline Trail/Bridger National Forest 1.8," etc. Climb northeast up a sage hill to the register box, then continue the steady climb to a vista of the aspen-filled Scab Creek Valley, Fremont Butte at 186°/SSE beneath the horizon, and the level plains beyond. Swing left through shady aspen and conifers at 0.3 mile and climb steeply again through sage. Soon glimpses of the Wyoming Range on the distant skyline west catch the eye: a snow-capped peak interrupts the long, blue range near McDougal Gap at 255°/W and 11,380-foot Wyoming Peak shows as a high point at 238°/WSW over 55 miles away. Curve left around the ridge to another view southwest of the valley, contour past a cabin ruin (left) at 0.8 mile, then pass through a barbed wire fence and soon fork left. Climb steeply through several switchbacks, bend right across tributaries after 1.1 miles, and make another steep climb. Eventually continue on the level, pass beneath an old beaver pond (left) at mile 1.7 where the view extends to a Toboggan Lake (right), and come to the National Forest boundary at 1.9 miles.

Contour at 6°/NNE onto a hillside of aspen clumps, passing conifer-encircled Boundaryline Lake (below right). Pass a less-noticeable, peanut-shaped lake (right) at 2.4 miles, wind through a grassy meadow to a double pond (left) at 2.7 miles, then drop past

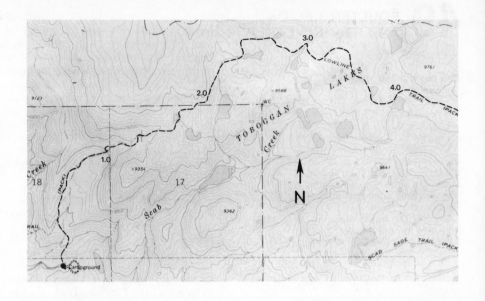

Lily pad ring on Toboggan Lake

an oval lake (right) at mile 3.0 and zig-zag southeast. Pass another lily-pad-covered pond (left) at 3.8 miles and wind east to the left side of Toboggan Lake at mile 4.0, marked by a sign. Climb and drop through rocks and scattered lodgepole pine, then drop into the head of the Scab Creek Valley and cross the Bridger Wilderness boundary at 4.8 miles. Eventually swing right across a tiny tributary, continue east along a drainage of willows and pine (right) then a marshy meadow, and come to Little Divide Lake and the Lowline Trail/Scab Creek Trail junction at mile 5.6.

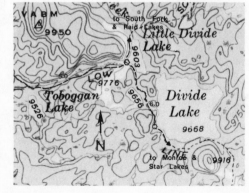

49 BOULTER, LEGION, AND FRANCIS LAKES

One day trip or backpack
Distances:
  Twin Lakes - 2.6 miles/4.2 KM.
  Boulter Lake - 4.1 miles/6.6 KM.
  Legion Lake - 5.5 miles/8.8 KM.
  Francis Lake - 6.0 miles/9.7 KM.
Hiking time: 3½ hours one way
Elevation gain: 970 feet/296 M.
Elevation loss: 530 feet/162 M.
Maximum elevation: 9,590 feet/2,923 M.
Season: Late June through mid-October
Topographic map:
  U.S.G.S. Big Sandy Opening, Wyo. 1969
Pinedale Ranger District
Bridger-Teton National Forest

Take this delightfully easy, rolling trail through the lowlands of the Bridger Wilderness in early summer when deep snows still make travel difficult in the alpine ranges east. Or enjoy its solitude in July and August when crowds of hikers clog the trail to Big Sandy Lake (No. 50). FISH: Brk in Boulter Lake; none in Legion Lake; Ct, Brk in Francis Lake.

From Pinedale drive southeast on U.S. 187 to the junction with Wyo. 353 at Boulder. Turn east, proceed past the Boulder Lake and Scab Creek turnoffs, and continue to the Big Sandy Junction, 19.3 miles — almost all paved — from U.S. 187. (A dirt road south of Boulder also connects U.S. 187 with Big Sandy Junction.) Turn left (east), drive another 9.0 miles to a left turn, stay right at 14.0 miles where the Muddy Ridge Road turns left, and come to the Big Sandy Entrance turnoff, 16.4 miles from Big Sandy Junction. Turn left (north) where the sign reads "Dutch Joe G.S. 3," etc. Cross the Bridger National Forest Boundary, pass turnoffs to Dutch Joe Guard Station, Sedgewick Meadow, and Big Sandy Lodge, and enter the Big Sandy Campground and parking area, 10.4 miles north of the Big Sandy Entrance turnoff.

For the quickest access from Big Sandy Campground, turn left (west) where a sign reads "Horse Corral/Unloading Ramp." Fork right after 25 yards past the corrals (left) and come to a sign at 0.1 mile, marking the "Meeks Lake Trail," etc. After a short climb through scattered pine, fork left (northwest) on the Meeks Lake Trail, soon turn right

(north) past the Fremont Spur Trail turnoff, and climb gradually up an open basin to the Highline Trail register at 1.1 miles. Fork left (northwest) into aspen where the right fork stays in the basin and wind on a slight climb past lookouts of the high, creviced range east, dominated by tilted, blunt-topped Temple Peak at 72°/E. Re-enter mixed conifers on a rolling climb, pass a Willow Creek pond (left) after 2.1 miles, and break from the shadows into a marshy basin, soon gaining a view again of the Temple Peak Range east.

Loop left then right past the north end of North Twin Lake after 2.7 miles, link openings in the conifers to another basin at mile 3.3, and begin dropping northwest down a Boulter Lake tributary. The trail swings right across the creek at mile 3.6 (a good water stop) and then recrosses Boulter Lake at mile 3.9 to intercept the Lowline Trail, marked by a sign but not visible on the ground. To proceed to Legion Lake, do not cross the creek at 3.9 miles: follow blazes and posts across another tributary on an 8°/NNE bearing and climb the hillside to a marshy meadow (right) at 4.1 miles. Bend left around the marsh to a tributary crossing at mile 4.7, pass a small pond and wind through high boulders, dropping into another long, marshy basin at 5.0 miles. Skirt the right side of the basin, following cairns and blazes again where the trail is indistinct, and climb up a short switchback after mile 5.4 to a view of Legion Lake.

Circle east of Legion Lake, stay high above a drainage (left), and wind north through conifers and boulders to Francis Lake at 6.0 miles. Here a cairn-marked sign indicates directions east to Fish Creek Park and west to East Fork River. To return to Big Sandy Campground from Francis Lake on a different — and scenic — route, take the trail east along Fish Creek to the open, rolling flats of Fish Creek Park. In view here are rocky, shadowed ranges from Wind River Peak at 92°/ESE north along the Continental Divide to Big Sandy Mountain at 45°/ENE. Turn south onto the Meeks Lake Trail (which also leads north to Dads and Marms Lakes) and make an easy climb to viewpoints of pointed Mt. Geikie at 321°/NNW and the Mt. Hooker amphitheater at 330°/NNW. Drop south above Meeks Lake Creek (left), pass the V Lake turnoff (No. 50) and Meeks Lake, and soon come to the Big Sandy Campground, 6.3 miles from Francis Lake.

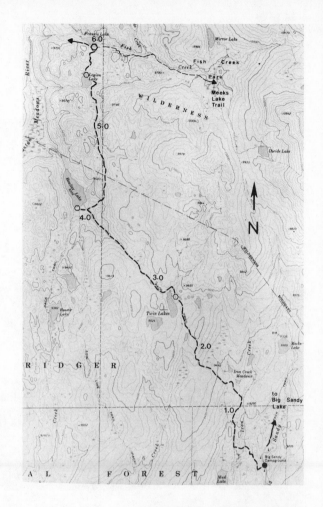

Boulder-strewn Fish Creek Park

Blue grouse

50 MEEKS, V, DIAMOND, AND BIG SANDY LAKES

One day trip or backpack
Distances:
  Meeks Lake - 1.3 miles/2.1 KM.
  V Lake - 2.1 miles/3.4 KM.
  Diamond Lake - 3.5 miles/5.6 KM.
  Big Sandy Lake - 6.0 miles/9.7 KM.
Hiking time: 3½ hours one way
Elevation gain: 860 feet/262 M.
Elevation loss: 240 feet/73 M.
Maximum elevation: 9,740 feet/2,969 M.
Season: July through early October
Topographic maps:
  U.S.G.S. Big Sandy Opening, Wyo. 1969
  U.S.G.S. Temple Peak, Wyo. 1969
Pinedale Ranger District
Bridger-Teton National Forest

Next to the Elkhart Park Entrance out of Pinedale, the Big Sandy Entrance near the southern end of the Bridger Wilderness receives the most visitors. They are drawn in large part by the decades of publicity given to Lonesome Lake (it's not) and the Cirque of Towers (yes, rugged . . . incredibly beautiful), reached in the Popo Agie Wilderness via Jackass Pass (SEE No. 61). Fishermen, technical climbers, day-hikers, and backpackers, many on their first trip into the Wind River Range, plod the dusty trail up the Big Sandy River Valley from early July through early September. Big game move out in the face of the annual development of tent suburbs, even in the alpine country around Black Joe, Deep, and Temple Lakes. Thus, for the lover of wilderness, this route cannot be tolerated until mid-September or so, after the first snow. During July and August, enter the Wilderness at the Scab Creek Entrance (see No. 48). FISH: Brk in Meeks Lake; Rbw in V Lake; Brk, Ct in Big Sandy Lake.

Drive to the Big Sandy Entrance southeast of Pinedale, following the directions for Boulter, Legion and Francis Lakes (No. 49).

Hike north from the campground on the Meeks Lake Trail, staying left of the Big Sandy River. Break from scattered trees into a spacious park where the view extends to the rocky knob of Laturio Mountain at 354°/N and soon come to the trail register. For the route past Meeks, V, and Diamond Lakes, stay left on the Meeks Lake Trail at 0.6 mile where the Big Sandy Trail forks right. Climb steadily then contour to a crossing of Meeks Lake Creek at 1.0 mile, pass right of round Meeks Lake, and fork right (north) at 1.4 miles onto the Diamond Lake Trail where the left fork proceeds to Dads Lake. Climb then drop over a slight saddle at 1.8 miles, circle the northwest side of V Lake and break out to beautiful views of the surrounding ranges. Steep, north-facing cliffs and rocky, alpine slopes rise toward the summit of Temple Peak at 92°/ESE and farther down the trail Laturio Mountain at 310°/NW and Schiestler Peak at 60°/ENE can be seen.

Follow posts through a series of parks and marshes where the trail is indistinct, cross a small rise after 3.3 miles, and penetrate thick conifers around the west side of Diamond Lake. Cross a meadow to the northeast end of the lake at 3.8 miles, rejoin the Big Sandy Trail near mile 4.0, and continue northeast up the small valley. Dip across small tributaries at 4.2, then 4.6 miles, crest over a slight hill at mile 4.8 where the Big Sandy River Valley shows right, and soon pass a marsh (right) which opens the view to pointed, scree-covered Big Sandy Mountain at 38°/NE. Stay in the trees past a swampy bog (left) at 5.3 miles and drop slightly to the southwest end of Big Sandy Lake at mile 5.6. Proceed over the grassy path around the west side of the lake, cross Lost Creek at 6.0 miles, and come to a trail junction at 6.2 miles. The panorama at this point includes most of the surrounding peaks: Schiestler Peak in the foreground at 154°/S, the sharp, west ridge of Temple Peak at 136°/SSE, the tilted summit of East Temple Peak at 118°/SE, the massive granite wall of Haystack Mountain at 93°/ESE, and the rounded, conifer-dotted side of Big Sandy Mountain at 51°/ENE.

From the junction of 6.2 miles, one trail climbs north, passes Arrowhead Lake after another 2.7 miles, then crosses Jackass Pass (also marked as Big Sandy Pass) at 3.0 miles and drops to Lonesome Lake beneath the Cirque of the Towers, 4.0 miles from the north side of Big Sandy Lake. Another trail circles Big Sandy Lake, crosses North and Black Joe Creeks, then forks west at mile 6.7 and climbs another 1.3 miles to Black Joe Lake. And from a third junction farther south at 6.9 miles, the Clear Lake Trail splits left, reaching Clear Lake in another 0.8 miles and Deep Lake in 2.2 miles while the Little Sandy Lake Trail stays right (south) to Rapid Lake, etc.

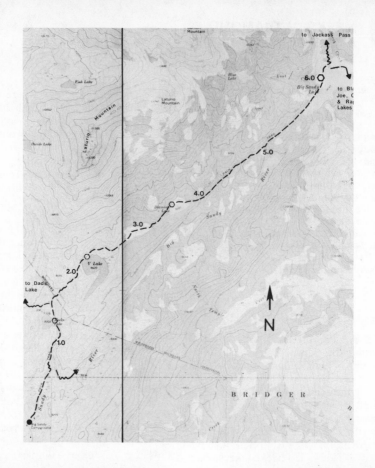

Big Sandy Mountain above Big Sandy Lake

Backpacking couple

Bear tracks

51 LITTLE SANDY LAKE

One day trip or backpack
Distance: 4.2 miles/6.8 KM. one way
Hiking time: 2½-3 hours one way
Elevation gain: 1,360 feet/415 M.
Elevation loss: 760 feet/232 M.
Maximum elevation: 10,140 feet/3,091 M.
Season: July through early October
Topographic maps:
   U.S.G.S. Sweetwater Needles, Wyo. 1969
   U.S.G.S. Sweetwater Gap, Wyo. 1953
Pinedale Ranger District
Bridger-Teton National Forest

Nestled within a conifer-and-scree bowl at the south end of the Wind River Range, Little Sandy Lake transmits an enticing mood of unspoiled, seldom-visited wilderness. The drive to the Sillwater Entrance is long and rough, and the trail, although well-maintained, climbs then drops on leg-burning pitches. But for the backpacker who seeks solitude or who wants a different approach to the Frozen Lakes/Big Sandy Lake country, this trail is highly recommended. FISH: Ct and Gryl.

Drive on U.S. 187 to the junction with Wyo. 353 at Boulder, 12 miles southeast of Pinedale. Turn east and proceed 19.3 miles — almost all paved — to the Big Sandy Junction, also accessible via dirt road south of Boulder. Turn left (east), continue another 9.0 to a left turn, stay right at 14.0 miles where the Muddy Ridge Road turns left, and come to the Big Sandy Entrance turnoff after 16.4 miles. Turn right, proceed another 5.6 miles to a left fork (the right fork provides access to Farson), fork left again at 10.3 miles, and follow signs marking "Sweetwater Guard Station" through several more turnoffs. After 18.9 miles from the Big Sandy Entrance turnoff, come to a right turn to "1 Sweetwater Campground" and a left turn to "Sweetwater Wilderness Entrance 6." Either find off-the-road parking here, or park in the campground, or take the left fork another 2 miles over considerably rougher road to parking near the trailhead.

From the "Sweetwater Wilderness Entrance 6" sign, begin hiking north-northwest up the rough jeep road. Continue the climb on the right fork where a left fork, marked "Lowline Tr.," contours through the sage, and follow the ridge above Sweetwater River, then Larsen Creek to the Little Sandy Lake Trailhead, the point from which mileage is figured for the information capsule. Stay left on a climb into lodgepole pine where the Sweetwater Gap Trail forks right, skirt the Larsen Creek basin just inside treeline for several hundred yards, and after 0.3 mile swing right across a marshy tributary toward a post at the far north end. Climb into pine again on the now-obvious trail, hop over a tributary of Larsen Creek near 0.9 mile and soon cross the signed Bridger Wilderness boundary. Continue the northerly course past sun-filled glens and open stands of pine, pass a swampy tributary after 1.2 miles and eventually climb to a slight ridge at 1.5 miles where the south summit of Mt. Nystrom shows through the trees at 340°/N.

Begin a steep, winding drop northwest to a crossing over Larsen Creek at 1.6 miles, contour above the creek past a tributary at 2.0 miles, then follow cairns and blazes on a climb into stands of gray-trunked limber pine. Again the scree hillside and high, khaki summit of Mt. Nystrom fill the tree openings right, now at a 1°/NNE bearing. Pass a left fork which rejoins the main trail in 25 yards, continue the steady climb up the Larsen Creek Valley and eventually climb up the bottom of the dry basin to a saddle at 3.1 miles, marked "Continental Divide." Crest over the saddle to a slight glimpse of Little Sandy Lake northwest and wind down a series of steep switchbacks, soon reaching a good lookout of the lake and the jagged, unnamed summits east of Independent Mountain at 319°/NNW.

Cross a tributary and after another steep descent, swing left from a sign reading "Little Sandy Lake," then contour beneath a rocky basin and follow the blazed trail on a final drop to the west side of the lake near the outlet. An interesting, 20-foot-high rock dam spans the creek here, remnants of a Civilian Conservation Corps project in the 1930's, and a tiny log cabin, hand-hewn about six logs high and sod-roofed, sits several yards north of the creek. Distances from the trail junction 0.2 miles below Little Sandy Lake to other destinations: North Frozen Lake via the Little Sandy Creek Trail — 5.9 miles, Temple Peak Saddle — 6.2 miles, Temple Lake — 7.0 miles, Miller Lake — 8.0 miles, Big Sandy Lake — 10.1 miles.

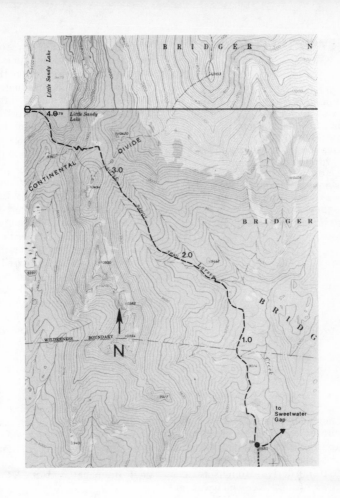

Rock-eroded petroglyph

121

52 SWEETWATER GAP

One day trip or backpack
Distance: 6.1 miles/9.8 KM. one way
Hiking time: 4-4½ hours one way
Elevation gain: 1,540 feet/469 M.
Elevation loss: 95 feet/29 M.
Maximum elevation: 10,327 feet/3,148 M.
Season: July through early October
Topographic maps:
  U.S.G.S. Sweetwater Needles, Wyo. 1969
  U.S.G.S. Sweetwater Gap, Wyo. 1953
Pinedale Ranger District
Bridger-Teton National Forest

The narrow, north-south saddle of Sweetwater Gap separates the Mt. Nystrom range (east) from Roaring Fork Mountain (west) at the south end of the Wind River Mountains. The name of the Gap derives from its association with the Sweetwater River which was said to have been named by Gen. William H. Ashley in 1823, because the water tasted sweet to his trappers in contrast to the bitter alkali water they had been drinking. French trappers called the river **Eau Sucree** or "sugar water," according to Mae Urbanek in *Wyoming Place Names*. Other accounts suggest that the name first originated with the Indians. In the early pioneer days the Sweetwater Gap served as the passageway for a much-used horse trail which linked the Big Sandy Area with Lander via the Middle Popo Agie River Valley.

Today the Sweetwater Entrance and Sweetwater Trail attract fewer hikers and backpackers than do the more developed Big Sandy and Fiddlers Lake Entrances. Thus, the solitude, the increased chance of seeing wildlife (elk, deer, coyote), and the intrigue of a passage through high, rugged peaks all make this route well-worthwhile, similar in appeal to the hike over Telephone Pass (No. 13) in the Wyoming Range. The Sweetwater Gap itself serves as a good destination for a long, one-day trip. Or, for an extended trip north into the heart of the Wind River Range, the Gap can be crossed and trails linked to the Ice and Deep Creek Lakes, the North Fork Popo Agie River via the Pinto Park Trail, South Fork and Washakie Lakes (No. 63) via the Lizard Head Trail, and Grave Lake (No. 64).

Drive to the Sweetwater Entrance near the south end of the Bridger Wilderness, following directions for Little Sandy Lake (No. 51).

From the "Sweetwater Wilderness Entrance 6" sign, hike (or drive) northwest up the rough jeep road for 2 miles to the Little Sandy Lake/Sweetwater Gap Trailhead, the point from which mileage is figured for the information capsule. Turn east on a gradual descent where the Little Sandy Lake Trail (No. 51) climbs north, ford Larsen Creek on a log at mile 0.1, and begin a steep, rolling climb northeast through dense lodgepole pine. Break from the trees near 1.0 mile to the first view of the high, rocky Mt. Nystrom saddle at 330°/NNW and cross the Bridger Wilderness boundary after another 100 yards. Swing right past a small pond (left) at 1.4 miles, pass another small, serene pool at mile 1.9 and wind northeast in and out of several grassy basins. Climb steadily up a forested ridge after 2.5 miles, cross a marshy tributary near mile 2.9 and continue on an easier climb across several small drainages and creeks, entering a narrower valley.

Cross a larger tributary at 4.4 miles which cascades through a rocky drainageway and step stones across the tiny Sweetwater River at mile 4.7, an opening from which the sharp summit of Mt. Nystrom can be seen at 260°/W. Climb north up the rocky path through limber pine and fire-burned snags, skirt a large meadow after 5.1 miles, and pass a beautiful vista of the "12004" summit at 264°/W with the steep, columned cirque below. Re-enter conifers and cross a tributary at 5.5 miles and make a final climb through the narrow valley floor to the broad saddle of Sweetwater Gap at mile 6.1, marked by a sign. From this high vantage the knobby, rock-and-conifer range around the Ice Lakes area fills the skyline north-northwest. The trail drops due north from Sweetwater Gap and reaches Tayo Park after another 2.0 miles, providing an alternate access to Tayo and Coon Lakes (No. 56), the Ice Lakes (No. 57), and the Deep Creek Lakes (No. 58).

122

Sun-struck columbine

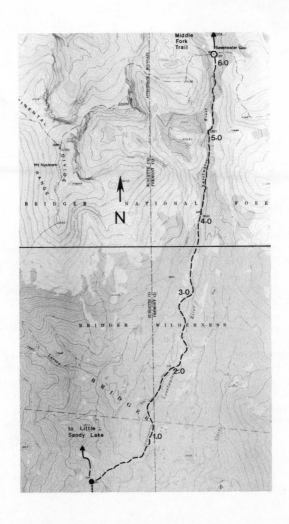

53 LOWER SILAS, TOMAHAWK, AND UPPER SILAS LAKES

One day trip
Distances:
Lower Silas Lake - 2.4 miles/3.9 KM.
Tomahawk Lake - 3.0 miles/4.8 KM.
Upper Silas Lake - 3.4 miles/5.5 KM.
Hiking time: 2-2½ hours one way
Elevation gain: 870 feet/265 M.
Elevation loss: 180 feet/55 M.
Maximum elevation: 10,100 feet/3,078 M.
Season: Late June through mid-September
Topographic maps:
U.S.G.S. Cony Mountain, Wyo. 1953
U.S.G.S. Christina Lake, Wyo. 1953
Lander Ranger District
Shoshone National Forest

Lower Silas, Tomahawk, and Upper Silas Lakes lie outside the Popo Agie Wilderness within the Little Popo Agie Basin at the south end of the Shoshone National Forest. Nestled in groves of fragrant pine, these lakes lack the stunning beauty and magnificent rock surroundings of the high alpine lakes within the Wilderness northwest. But they remain quite popular with local fishermen, groups like the Boy Scouts, and families with young children, due to their quick and easy access and usual good fishing conditions. Until the Wilderness boundary would be changed to include this area, motor bikes might be encountered on the trails. Silas Canyon, west of Upper Silas Lake, marks the beginning of the austere, alluring high country, a distinct contrast to the wooded hillsides and more peaceful lakes below. Glacier-carved, strewn with boulders, covered with shallow lakes and willow basins, it makes an excellent place for a day of exploring. Rock climbers could scale the west canyon wall, cross the top of Roaring Fork Mountain, and drop into the equally-rugged

Stough Creek Basin (see No. 54). FISH: Ct in Tomahawk Lake; Brk in Lower and Upper Silas Lakes.

From Wyo. 28 at the south end of the Shoshone National Forest, turn north onto the Louis Lake Road and proceed past the Louis Lake and Popo Agie Campgrounds to the Fiddlers Lake Campground. From Lander drive on the Sinks Canyon and Louis Lake Roads to the Worthen Meadow Reservoir turnoff, as described for Twin "Buzz" Lakes (No. 55). Stay left where the Worthen Meadow Reservoir Road forks right, proceed another 5.9 miles over Blue Ridge to the Fiddlers Lake Campground turnoff, then fork right and continue another 0.8 mile to the turn-around loop and parking area.

Bear southwest across the small meadow next to the parking area to a trailhead sign. Follow the Christina Lake Trail into black-trunked lodgepole pine, bend left and cross Fiddlers Creek after 0.3 mile, and continue past a marsh (right). Climb west to a ridgetop at 0.6 mile, begin a slight descent into thick trees again near 1.0 mile, then cross three tributaries of Silas Creek after 1.2 miles and resume the easy hillside climb. Near mile 1.6 come to the signed Silas Lake Trail: fork right (west) where the Christina Lake Trail, an alternate route, turns left (southwest). Climb gradually past a stand of dead timber (left), traverse a slight ridge after 1.8 miles, and soon swing left near Silas Creek and come to the Lower Silas Lake turnoff at mile 2.2 (see map).

To proceed to Tomahawk and Upper Silas Lakes, fork right across Silas Creek, climb northwest along a high ridge of boulders, and contour for several hundred yards along a tributary (right). Break into the open park around Silas Creek after 2.7 miles, bend left into pine again along the park (right), and after 50 yards come to a sign marking the Tomahawk Lake turnoff. Stay right again to get to Upper Silas Lake; continue northwest through pine along Silas Creek (right) and after 3.3 miles bend slightly left and come to a beautiful view across 100 yards of meadow of Upper Silas Lake. The use trail into Silas Canyon, unmarked on the U.S.G.S. topo but drafted in part onto the map photo, angles left from the lake trail at the far west corner of Upper Silas Lake. It then swings left (west) before crossing the creek and climbs from one plateau to the next along the south side of the Silas Canyon.

Raft fisherman on Upper Silas Lake

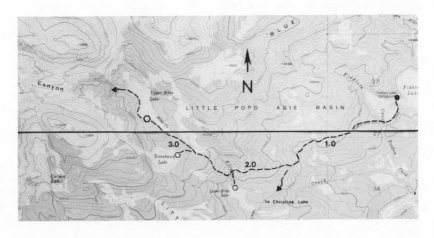

54 STOUGH CREEK LAKES

Backpack
Distance: 6.8 miles/10.9 KM. one way
Hiking time: 4½-5 hours one way
Elevation gain: 2,250 feet/686 M.
Elevation loss: 620 feet/189 M.
Maximum elevation: 10,550 feet/3,216 M.
Season: Late June through September
Topographic maps:
U.S.G.S. Cony Mountain, Wyo. 1953
U.S.G.S. Sweetwater Gap, Wyo. 1953
Lander Ranger District
Shoshone National Forest

In the early 1900's Charley Stough, for whom the Stough Creek Lakes are named, served as sheriff of Lander, then a bustling pioneer town of about 1200. A fair man but "tough as nails," Stough is best remembered for his capture of a drifter named Keefer who had murdered and robbed an old sheep herder near the Big Bend Roadhouse east of Lander. Sheriff Stough and Deputy Sheriff Allie Axe pursued Keefer almost to the Montana border before they apprehended him. When the three returned to Lander, a jury was quickly assembled, Keefer was found guilty and was sentenced to hang. The year was 1903, and the incident was thought to be the first **legal** hanging in Lander.

As with the Ice Lakes area (No. 57), an enticing feature of the Stough Creek Basin is its pristine alpine lakes and sheer, glacier-carved amphitheaters which lie beyond the sub-alpine lakes. Plan on three or four days for the trip and for a loop return, take the less-traveled Stough Creek Trail to the Twin "Buzz" Lakes (No. 55). FISH: Ct, Brk 13" in Big and Little Stough and Shoal Lakes; Ct 13" in Cutthroat, Footprint, and Blackrock Lakes; Brk in Lower and Upper Toadstool Lakes; none in Palette, Dipper, Eyrie, Zig-zag, Lightening, and Canyon Lakes (see map).

Drive on U.S. 287 into the middle of Lander, turn onto the Sinks Canyon Road/Wyo. 13, and proceed southwest along the Middle Popo Agie River to the Shoshone National Forest, 9.4 miles from U.S. 287. Pass the Sinks Canyon Campground, swing left across the Middle Popo Agie River, and switch-

back up Fossil Hill via the Louis Lake Road. Proceed past Frye Reservoir and fork right (west) after another 1.4 miles where a sign reads "Worthen Meadow Reservoir 2." Pass the signed Sheep Bridge Trail turnoff and continue south of Worthen Meadow Reservoir to the signed Roaring Fork Lake Trailhead, 2.5 miles from the Louis Lake Road. Park at a reservoir campsite or in the turn-around loop west of the reservoir.

Begin hiking southwest up a rocky, jeep-size road, marked "Roaring Fork Lake ½ mile." Climb steadily through several winds to more level terrain, bend right past Roaring Fork Lake (left) after 0.6 mile, then cross the outlet creek on logs 25 yards below the trail and climb back to the trailhead register and mileage signs. Climb west again on a rocky, single-lane path to a ridgetop and fork left onto corduroy past a marsh (right) near 0.9 mile. Break out of trees across a creek at 1.3 miles, pass an open park (left), then swing left past another opening (right) and cross 40 yards of corduroy. Bend left on a gradual climb, soon pick up a creek (left), and wind west on a steady climb. Eventually cross a tributary, then swing left across the main creek and link open meadows to an open alpine saddle at mile 3.4. Here the view encompasses the northern end of Roaring Fork Mountain at 210°/SW, then sweeps right to the high point of 13,400-foot Wind River Peak at 263°/W amid other cirques and summits on the high Continental Divide range.

Swing left from the saddle to a contour across the rocky hillside, soon enter conifers and begin a steady, winding drop to a main creek crossing at mile 4.6. Climb and drop over a slight rise, pass another marsh over several yards of corduroy, and cross the Popo Agie Wilderness boundary at 5.4 miles. Soon pass two marshy ponds (left), drop slightly to the right of the outlet creek and come to a junction at 5.7 miles with the Stough Creek Trail and Middle Fork Cutoff Trail. Cross the bridge over Stough Creek, a point which gives view to the 11,546-foot scree summit of Roaring Fork Mountain at 195°/SSW; swing left above the creek (right), and after mile 6.2 make a steady, ridgetop climb through limber pine. Break into more scattered trees near 6.6 miles as the climb lessens, and in several hundred more yards either fork left on a contour to the north end of Big Stough Lake or stay right and proceed toward the other Stough Creek Lakes (see map).

126

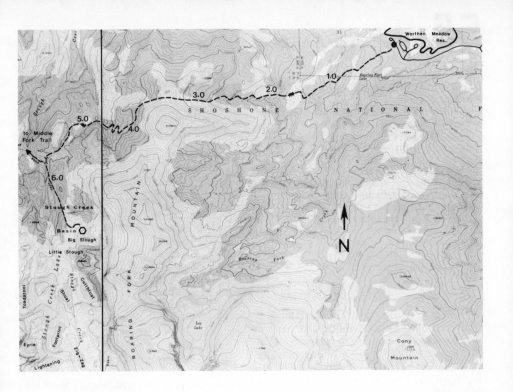

Stough Creek Basin

Marsh corduroy

55 TWIN "BUZZ" LAKES

One day trip or backpack
Distances:
  Middle Fork Trail - 2.0 miles/3.2 KM.
  East Twin Lake - 3.7 miles/6.0 KM.
  West Twin Lake - 4.1 miles/6.6 KM.
Hiking time: 2-2½ hours one way
Elevation gain: 765 feet/233 M.
Elevation loss: 635 feet/194 M.
Maximum elevation: 9,080 feet/2,768 M.
Season: Mid-June through September
Topographic map:
  U.S.G.S. Cony Mountain, Wyo. 1953
Lander Ranger District
Shoshone National Forest

Two main trails provide access from the Sinks Canyon/Louis Lake Road to the beautiful granite peaks and alpine high country of the Popo Agie (Po-POZ-yuh) Wilderness along the Continental Divide farther west. The Middle Fork Trail begins near the Middle Fork bridge above Bruce Picnic Ground, soon passes the scenic Popo Agie Falls, and winds west above the sparkling Middle Popo Agie River. Although this trail is usually traveled by horsepackers more than by backpackers due to length and elevation gain, it does make an excellent hike in early season when snow and mud cover the high routes. The Sheep Bridge Trail from Deer Park north of Worthen Meadow Reservoir (not to be confused with Deer Park east of Christina Lake) follows a mostly-downhill route into the Middle Popo Agie Valley, short-cutting 6.5 miles of the lower Middle Fork Trail. It joins the Middle Fork Trail beyond Sheep Bridge and then leads west toward Tayo Park, Poison and Coon Lakes (No. 56), Ice Lakes (No. 57), and Deep Creek Lakes (No. 58).

Sheep Bridge and East and West Twin Lakes are easily within range of a one-day trip. The lakes — shallow, green from marsh grass, with a sleepy-afternoon atmosphere — might also serve as a first-night's camp on a longer trip. They are unnamed on the 1953 U.S.G.S. topo as opposed to the trio of "Twin Lakes" on Petes Lake Trail about 2½ miles north, and the trail from Sheep Bridge on, although a clear path, is currently neither signed, blazed, nor plotted on the topo. Points of historical interest: In Crow Indian language, **Popo**

means "head" or "beginning," **Agie** mean "river"; hence, Popo Agie translates a "headwaters." The Popo Agie Rive "Sinks," passed on the drive through the Middle Popo Agie Canyon, are an interesting geological phenomenon where the river dis appears abruptly into a mountainside caver and emerges in a pond a half-mile below Stocked in the pond are "whopper" trout definitely worth the stop to see. Sheep Bridge constructed in 1926 by the Forest Service fo stockmen, was part of a Stock Driveway which linked Shoshone Lake and Dickinso Park with the Beavers Creek area. The Twin Lakes are known locally and unofficially a "Buzz Lakes" for "Buzz" Darlington o Lander who stocked them with trout "way back when." FISH: Brk.

Drive on U.S. 287 into the middle o Lander, turn onto the Sinks Canyo Road/Wyo. 13, and proceed southwest along the Middle Popo Agie River to the Shoshone National Forest, 9.4 miles from U.S. 287. Pass the Sinks Canyon Campground, then the Bruce Picnic Ground, and continue anothe 0.1 mile to the Middle Fork Trailhead — an alternate access — just before the bridge ove the Middle Popo Agie River. Switchback up Fossil Hill via the Louis Lake Road, pass Frye Reservoir, and fork right (west) after anothe 1.4 miles where a sign reads "Worthe Meadow Reservoir 2." Pass the Fremon County Youth Camp turnoff and turn righ (north) where a sign reads "Sheep Bridge Tra 2," 1.3 miles from the Louis Lake Road. Con tinue on the rough dirt road as far as safely possible: cross the narrow bridge over Roar ing Fork Creek, wind north and west through timbered areas and open parks, and park in o before Deer Park (see map).

At the west end of Deer Park pass the trailhead register and climb northwest beneath a shady canopy of pine to a slight saddle a mile 0.4. Begin a steep drop into the Middle Fork basin, swing left after 1.3 miles across a tributary, and wind over the valley floor past a small pond (right). After another steady drop over the rocky trail, break onto a sage knoll swing left and continue toward Sheep Bridge at 1.8 miles. Do not cross the bridge but stay on the south side and pick up the use trai which winds west-southwest. Climb into a drainage after 2.3 miles, wind southwest up a steep ridge, cross the creek at mile 2.9, and stay inside treeline on a more gradual climb to East Twin Lake at 3.7 miles. West Twin Lake lies another half-mile west.

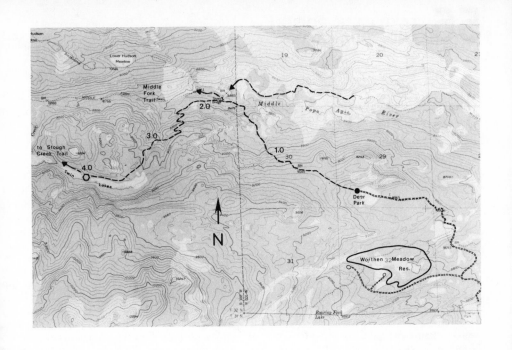

Porcupine

Backpack
Distances:
  Tayo Park - 9.3 miles/15.0 KM.
  Poison Lake - 11.1 miles/27.5 KM.
  Coon Lake - 13.3 miles/21.4 KM.
Hiking time: 7½-8½ hours one way
Elevation gain: 2,215 feet/675 M.
Elevation loss: 925 feet/282 M.
Maximum elevation: 10,535 feet/3,211 M.
Season: Early July through mid-September
Topographic maps:
  U.S.G.S. Cony Mountain, Wyo. 1953
  U.S.G.S. Sweetwater Gap, Wyo. 1953
Lander Ranger District
Shoshone National Forest

The Middle Fork Trail, one of the oldest in the area, dates back to the pioneer days of the late 1800's, then called the Sweetwater Trail. It proceeds west from Sheep Bridge (see No. 55), passes turnoffs to the Shoshone Lake Trail and the Pinto Park Trail to the Deep Creek Lakes (No. 58), and soon begins a bend southwest. Here the scenic Middle Popo Agie Valley widens, and the river, running wide and slow, meanders through a series of grassy, sun-filled parks. After an easy, rolling climb in and out of the pine which border these parks, the Middle Fork Trail passes a turnoff to the Stough Creek Lakes (No. 54) and at Tayo Park (correctly placed on the map) turns south toward Sweetwater Gap (No. 52), an alternate access. From Tayo Park the Tayo Lake Trail climbs northwest to the Ice Lakes Trail junction, then forks southwest into the Tayo Creek Valley. Ultimate destinations: Mountain Sheep and Little Mountain Sheep Lakes, Lower and Upper Tayo Lakes, Coon Lake, all couched within rugged, alpine cirques near the Continental Divide.

With a glance at the U.S.G.S. topo maps, the trails can easily be arranged into a series of loop trips, excellent options for backpack excursions of varying legnth. One recommended five- or six-day trip: Deer Park Entrance to Gill Park or Bills Park via Middle Fork Trail; to base camp near Salt Cache Park then on to Poison, Mountain Sheep, Coon, or Tayo Lakes via Tayo Lake Trail; to Ice Lakes via Ice Lakes Trail; to Deep Creek Lakes; back to Deer Park via Pinto Park or Deep Creek Trails. FISH: Ct, Gdn, Rbw, X's of those, Brk in Poison Lake; Ct, Gdn, X's 13" in Mountain Sheep Lake; none in Little Mountain Sheep Lake; Ct, Gdn, X's in Coon Lake; none in Lower and Upper Tayo Lakes.

From Lander drive on the Sinks Canyon and Louis Lake Roads to the Worthen Meadow Reservoir turnoff. Continue toward Deer Park north of Worthen Meadow Reservoir, following the driving instructions for Twin "Buzz" Lakes (No. 55).

Hike northwest from Deer Park on the winding descent into the Middle Popo Agie Valley, as given in No. 55. Swing right over Sheep Bridge at 1.8 miles where the Twin Lakes Trail stays south of the Middle Popo Agie River, and in another 25 yards intercept the well-signed Middle Fork Trail. Contour west past the Shoshone Lake Trail turnoff at 2.2 miles and climb gradually through aspen, pine and sage, passing cascades in the river (left). Cross two tributaries, enter thicker trees, then pass glimpses of deep pools in the river near miles 4.0 and follow the level path across other tributaries to the Wilderness boundary at 4.5 miles. To proceed on the Middle Fork Trail, stay left in 200 more yards where the Pinto Park Trail — an access for a longer, more adventurous loop — turns right. Weave through scattered pine past the open Three Forks Park left, wade the 30-foot-wide Middle Popo Agie River near 4.9 miles, and stay right past an unmarked trail to Stough Creek and Twin Lakes (see map). Curve south through switchbacks to Gill Park, 6.0 miles from the Deer Park Entrance. Here the view extends to sheer, snow-blanketed cliffs and rounded peaks at 193°/SSW and 208°/SW, part of the Mt. Nystrom range.

Skirt left of mirror-smooth pools of water in Bills Park after 7.4 miles. Bear west at mile 8.2 where the Stough Creek Cutoff — another loop option — climbs southeast, then climb and drop across Basco Creek after 8.6 miles and climb to Tayo Park at mile 9.3 where the Middle Fork Trail forks south toward Sweetwater Gap. Re-cross the river, pass a Wilderness Ranger Camp which is usually based in the trees north of the park, and make a short, steep climb to Salt Cache Park at 9.8 miles. Here the Tayo Lake Trail forks west, winding through limber pine to the shallow, wide Poison Lake at 11.1 miles, then leading to the Mountain Sheep Lake Trail turnoff at 11.9 miles and the Tayo Lake turnoff just past Tayo Creek at 12.0 miles. Coon Lake lies in a spectacular rock-studded basin another mile west.

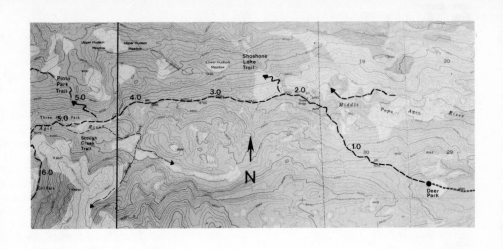

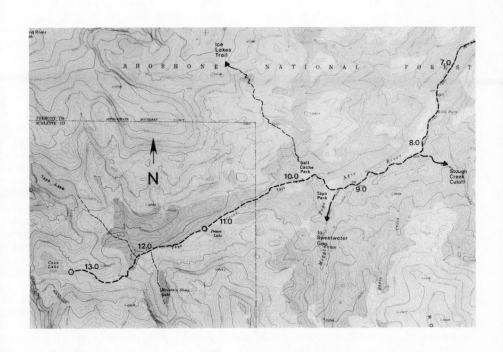

57 ICE LAKES

Backpack
Distance: (from Deer Park Entrance)
  Boot Lake - 12.9 miles/20.8 KM.
Hiking time: 7½-8½ hours one way
Elevation gain: 3,115 feet/949 M.
Elevation loss: 1,585 feet/483 M.
Maximum elevation: 10,980 feet/3,347 M.
Season: Early July through mid-September
Topographic maps:
  U.S.G.S. Cony Mountain, Wyo. 1953
  U.S.G.S. Sweetwater Gap, Wyo. 1953
Lander Ranger District
Shoshone National Forest

East of majestic Wind River Peak, highest summit in the south Wind River Range, a spattering of alpine lakes and tarns fills the many glacial cirques and bowls, much like the Stough Creek Lakes (No. 54) beneath Roaring Fork Mountain. The landscape here is cold and austere: light-colored granite boulders mix with the grasses and wildflowers of the tundra and patches of wind-stunted juniper and limber pine cling to the hillsides. The water in these exquisite lakes is crystal-pure and icy, snowfed throughout most of the summer. To get away from the mainstream of traffic through this area, climb west into the less-explored drainages of Fox, Little Walled, and Walled Lakes or Warbonnet and Boulder Lakes. Camp without a trace in this fragile alpine environment; pack out all litter. FISH: Brk, Gdn (a few) in Boot and Jug Lakes; none in Timberline, Fox, Little Walled and Walled

Lakes, none in Chief, Warbonnet, and Boulder Lakes (see map).

From Lander drive on the Sinks Canyon and Louis Lake Roads to the Worthen Meadow Reservoir turnoff. Continue toward Deer Park north of Worthen Meadow Reservoir, following the driving instructions for Twin "Buzz" Lakes (No. 55).

First, hike north from the Sweetwater Entrance through Sweetwater Gap (No. 52) to the Ice Lakes Trail junction east of Salt Cache Park. Or hike west and southwest from the Deer Park Entrance on the Sheep Bridge and Middle Fork Trails to the Ice Lakes Trail junction, the route figured for mileage and described in Tayo Park, Poison, and Coon Lakes (No. 56). Near the southeast corner of the park at mile 9.8 turn right (northwest) onto the Ice Lakes Trail where the Tayo Lake Trail proceeds west, a fork marked by signs. Stay right of the tributary which flows through the park, enter conifers and begin a steep, northerly climb. Cross a small tributary, climb right of the drainage through limber pine, then swing left past a small, swampy pond near 10.4 miles and continue the steep climb northwest to a saddle at 10.9 miles. This high lookout point gives a good view south of the country just crossed: the high plateau dotted with ponds at 122°/SE and the forested Middle Popo Agie Valley beyond.

Drop northwest to the crossing of an unnamed creek at 11.2 miles, follow cairns north and contour around a pond (left). Climb steeply again through short switchbacks and break from wind-stunted pine on a climb to another saddle at 11.8 miles. Here the panorama behind takes in the steep-sided canyon and rolling summits of Roaring Fork Mountain at 120°/SE, the obvious opening of Sweetwater Gap at 145°/SSE, and the rugged cirque above Little Mountain Sheep Lake in Mt. Nystrom at 177°/SSW. Cross the saddle onto a hillside contour north, now gaining an expansive view of the Ice Lakes cluster. Lofty Timberline Lake can be seen in the valley at 275°/W, the sheer, often-snow-covered cirque above Little Walled and Walled Lakes forms a backdrop farther west, and Boot Lake, then Jug Lake catch the sun at 334°/N. Drop steadily north and northwest down the hillside, cross a swale at 12.3 miles, then begin another drop past the steep rock wall above Warbonnet Lake and come to two outlet creeks from Chief Lake at mile 12.9. See the map for trails to the other lakes.

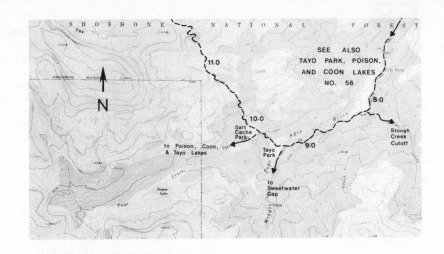

Creek crossing

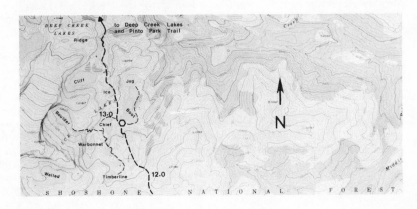

58 DEEP CREEK LAKES

Backpack
Distance: (from Deer Park Entrance)
   Lower Deep Cr. Lk. - 12.1 miles/19.5 KM.
Hiking time: 7-8 hours one way
Elevation gain: 2,820 feet/860 M.
Elevation loss: 1,530 feet/466 M.
Maximum elevation: 10,600 feet/3,231 M.
Season: Early July through mid-September
Topographic maps:
   U.S.G.S. Cony Mountain, Wyo. 1953
   U.S.G.S. Sweetwater Gap, Wyo. 1953
   U.S.G.S. Moccasin Lake, Wyo. 1937*
     *15 minute series
Lander Ranger District
Shoshone National Forest

Rarified tundra and deep conifer forests . . . large, pristine alpine lakes . . . many subalpine lakes with excellent fishing conditions . . . habitat for mule deer, elk, and many small mammals . . . all these enticing qualities characterize the Deep Creek Lakes area north of the Ice Lakes. Take the high route through Pinto Park — figured for the information capsule and described below — for a grand vista of Lizard Head Peak and the Cirque of the Towers near mile 9.4 and for a trail link into the North Fork Popo Agie Valley. Or follow the low route through the Deep Creek Valley for an easier climb to the trout-filled lakes. FISH: Brk in Pinto Park, Park, Heart, Lower and Upper Baer, Lower and Upper Echo Lakes; Gdn 12" in Lower Deep Creek Lake; none in Middle and Upper Deep Creek Lakes.

From Lander drive on the Sinks Canyon and Louis Lake Roads to the Worthen Meadow Reservoir turnoff. Continue toward Deer Park north of Worthen Meadow Reservoir, following the driving instructions for Twin "Buzz" Lakes (No. 55).

Follow the Sheep Bridge Trail northwest from Deer Park on a steady drop into the Middle Popo Agie Valley and then hike west on the Middle Fork Trail to the Pinto Park Trail turnoff near mile 4.6, according to directions in No. 55 and No. 56. Fork right (north) onto the signed Pinto Park Trail, begin climbing the rocky, aspen-covered hillside, and soon proceed through short switchbacks. Come to viewpoints of the winding rolls of Middle Popo Agie River in Three Forks Park below, the northern, alpine end of Roaring Fork Mountain at 141°/SSE, and the Mt. Nystrom range flanked by a steep, triangular summit at 195°/SSW. Wind west and northwest as the grade moderates after 5.2 miles, skirt the edge of a marsh and continue through deadfall fire-blackened snags and pine. Contour over near-level trail, looping around another marsh on a 15-foot corduroy. Cross two tributaries, switchback to a good view of Wind River Peak — flanked by a snowfield — at 232°/WSW and break into the small opening of Kenny Wood Park after 7.3 miles.

Follow the scenic trail in and out of small clearings, cross two, then a third bridge tributaries, and near mile 7.9 come to the signed Deep Creek Lakes Cutoff (see map). To continue on the Pinto Park Trail, fork right along the ridgetop where the Cutoff Trail drops left. Climb steadily across more tributaries and into thicker spruce and pine, then after 8.7 miles contour into the lower end of Pinto Park. Follow treeline past the grassy basin (left) and curve north to a grand vista of majestic Wind River Peaks near mile 9.4. From here the familiar shape of Lizard Head Peak can be seen on the skyline at 278°/WNW east of the sharp pinnacles that comprise the famous Cirque of the Towers (see No. 61). Look for cairns near the upper end of Pinto Park where the trail is indistinct, drop steeply northwest to a crossing of Baer Lakes Creek at mile 10.1, and reach the signed Ice Lakes Trail/North Fork Popo Agie Trail Cutoff junction in another 20 yards.

Fork left (south-southwest) onto the Ice Lakes Trail, climb steadily up the valley through spruce and fir, and break to a view of Lower Baer Lake near 10.5 miles. Wind south past this lake, then past Upper Baer Lake at mile 10.8, climb past a scenic rock wall (east) which borders the valley, and cross a ridge to the rock-enclosed Lower and Upper Echo Lakes at 11.3 miles. Switchback up the hillside south of Upper Echo Lake to a beautiful panoramic vista of cirque walls and rocky peaktops northwest, then cross the ridgetop to a view south of Lower Deep Creek Lake and the granite wall at 240°/WSW above unseen Middle Deep Creek Lake. Drop gradually southeast to Lower Deep Creek Lake at mile 12.1 and come to an unsigned fork several hundred yards east where the Deep Creek Lake Trail loops east down Deep Creek to Heart and other lakes (see map) and the Ice Lakes Trail climbs south to the Ice Lakes (No. 57).

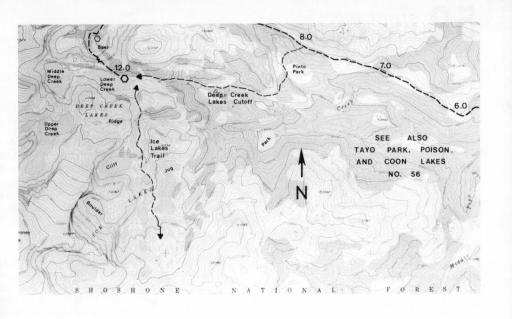

SEE ALSO
TAYO PARK, POISON,
AND COON LAKES
NO. 56

Deep Creek Lake landscape

59 SMITH, MIDDLE, CATHEDRAL, AND COOK LAKES

Backpack:

Distances:
  Smith Lake - 6.0 miles/9.7 KM.
  Middle Lake - 6.5 miles/10.5 KM.
  Cathedral Lake - 7.5 miles/12.1 KM.
  (Cook Lake - 7.3 miles/11.7 KM.)
Hiking time: 4½-5 hours one way
Elevation gain: 1,350 feet/411 M.
Elevation loss: 650 feet/198 M.
Maximum elevation: 10,100 feet/3,078 M.
Season: Late June through September
Topographic map:
  U.S.G.S. Moccasin Lake, Wyo. 1937*
    ***15 minute series**
Lander Ranger District
Shoshone National Forest

A double chain of paternoster lakes, hidden within unnamed summits southeast of Cathedral Peak, spill east into Smith Lake Creek. With a myriad granite spires and glacier-polished outcroppings, embellished by scattered stands of lodgepole and limber pine, they make very appealing destinations for three-and four-day trips, similar in setting to Ross and Louise Lakes (No's. 32 and 33) in the Fitzpatrick Wilderness. Especially stunning is the massive rock spire which soars above Cathedral Lake, seen also from Middle Lake at 278°/WNW. For solitude, avoid the lakeshore camping sites around Smith, Middle, Cathedral, and Cook. Plan your overnight stay for the deep, pristine valleys south of Mt. Chauvenet, below Upper Cathedral, or below Glacier and Phyllis Lakes. FISH: Brk, Mcknw in Smith, Middle, and Cathedral Lakes; Brk in Cook, Phyllis, and Glacier; none in Upper Cathedral Lake.

Turn west from U.S. 287 onto the unmarked Moccasin Lake Road at Hine's General Store, 16.5 miles north of Lander (the Lander Valley High School) and 15.6 miles south of the U.S. 26 junction. Proceed to the end of the paved road at 5.3 miles, climb over the narrow, well-maintained gravel road through even switchbacks up Bald Mountain, and stay left as the Moccasin Lake Road turns right, 19.8 miles from U.S. 287. Continue south another

1.7 miles past the Bears Ears Trailhead turn, pass the Dickinson Creek Campground at 3.? miles, and come to the North Fork and Smith Lake Trailhead and nearby parking area at 4.? miles.

Drop several yards to the marsh around Twin Parks Creek, bear 146°/SSE for about 200 yards across the marsh corduroy, and wind right then left to a climb up the hillside. Enter conifers, pick up the old jeep road which joins left, and near 0.3 mile come to a sign reading "Smith Lake Trail/North Fork Trail." Fork right onto the Smith Lake Trail, follow pine blazes to a switchbacking climb through a slight saddle between knolls, and eventually contour onto a hillside where the view opens for the first time. The rocky 10,873-foot mountaintop west of unseen Shoshone Lake shows at 142°/SSE, and the vista extends right to the 11,038-foot mountain at 170°/S west of Mt. Chevo. After a slight drop with a bend left then right, the trail leads to another vista, screened by trees. Four snow-filled cirques with steep, creviced walls distinguish an unnamed Continental Divide peak at 190°/SSW, between Wind River and Big Sandy Peaks.

Descend southwest through over a dozen winding switchbacks, drop across a creek after 2.8 miles which marks the first water of the trip, then pass the Wilderness Area boundary and skirt below the 1952 Dishpan Fire Area. The huge rock knob of Dishpan Butte shows above the burned snags and seedling pine north. And soon the granite-topped mountains west of Cathedral and Glacier Lakes, one at 287°/WNW, rise into view above the treetops. Eventually loop around a large meadow (left) to the signed junction with the High Meadow Trail near 4.5 miles, an alternate route to Cliff and High Meadow Lake (No. 60). Stay right on the near-level trail, parallel a rock wall seen through the trees farther right, then enter thicker conifers and break to a view of Smith Lake at mile 5.7. Climb steadily up the rock-and-conifer hillside north of the lake, bend left across Smith Lake Creek, and come to the Cook Lake Trail junction at 6.3 miles. Stay right and break out to the southeast side of scenic Middle Lake in another 100 yards. To get to Cathedral Lake, loop around the north "toe" of Middle Lake, turn right onto a cairn-marked trail and climb steeply, then contour west.

For the hike to Cook Lake, fork left at the

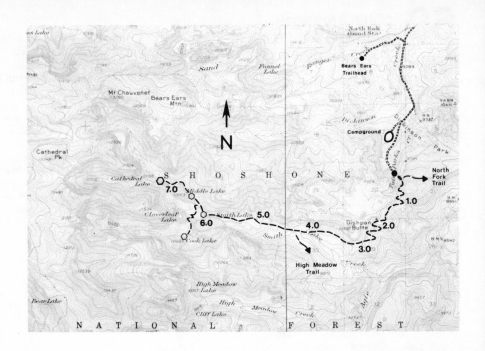

Spire above Cathedral Lake

junction at 6.3 miles, cross the outlet from Middle Lake, and wind from 140°/SSE to 222°/SW to the outlet from Cloverleaf Lake, half-hidden within a rugged bowl (right). Climb through limber pine and drop over a ridge, head toward a rock wall on the skyline, then make a final drop right to the north shore of Cook Lake.

60 CLIFF AND HIGH MEADOW LAKES

Backpack
Distances: 8.9 miles/14.3 KM. one way
Hiking time: 5½-6 hours one way
Elevation gain: 1,805 feet/550 M.
Elevation loss: 1,150 feet/351 M.
Maximum elevation: 10,055 feet/3,065 M.
Season: Late June through September
Topographic map:
 U.S.G.S. Moccasin Lake, Wyo. 1937*
  ***15 minute series**
Lander Ranger District
Shoshone National Forest

As with the Smith, Middle, Cathedral, and Cook Lakes hike (No. 59), the trip to the exquisite, glacier-carved bowls of Cliff and High Meadow Lakes begins from the North Fork and Smith Lake Trailhead. This starting point southwest of Dickinson Park, and the nearby Bears Ears Trailhead south of Funnel Creek provide the main access into that part of the Popo Agie Wilderness south of the Wind River Indian Reservation. While the North Fork Trail follows a slightly longer and easier route, with proximity to fly-fishing and nicely-hidden camping sites along the North Fork Popo Agie River, the Bears Ears Trail (see No. 62) figures as the shorter, despite interminable switchbacks. But both routes lead west into the heart of the Wind River Range where 12,000-foot spires and peaks—much more rugged and spectacular from this east side than from the west side of the Bridger Wilderness — mark the skyline. U.S.G.S. topographic maps in the 7.5 minute series will be available for this area by 1981, replacing the badly out-of-date Moccasin Lake topo.

Include a sidetrip to Cliff and High Meadow Lakes as part of a week-long journey to Lonesome, South Fork, and Grave Lakes, etc. Or take several days and explore well the High Meadow Creek Valley, stopping also at Gray, Shelf, and Sheep Lakes. FISH: Ct 12''.

Turn west from U.S. 287 north of Lander and proceed on the Moccasin Lake Road to the North Fork and Smith Lake Trailhead, following the directions given for No. 59.

Cross the corduroy and follow the clear trail south to the Smith Lake and North Fork Trail junction at 0.3 mile. Fork left onto the North Fork Trail where the Smith Lake Trail bears right, and wind southeast and east through blazed pine. After about 1.5 miles curve right and begin a series of switchbacks down the rocky, south-facing mountainside, passing glimpses of the unnamed, glacier-cut peak at 199°/SW on the Continental Divide. Eventually bend left at 104°/ESE, break onto an open, rock hillside where the view extends toward Big Sandy Mountain above the forested North Fork Popo Agie basin, then reenter trees and make another switchbacking drop. Cross and re-cross a tributary near 2.5 miles, drop to another tributary crossing after mile 2.7 and break onto a sage bench where the Shoshone Lake Trail forks left. Climb gradually through towering, red-barked pine, now within sound of the North Fork Popo Agie River (left), and after mile 4.0 cross the Popo Agie Wilderness boundary.

Turn left, soon ford the river, and continue on a gradual, then steeper climb along the southeast valleyside. Eventually contour again to river level, break out of conifers to a view ahead of Sanford Park near 5.4 miles and make a careful second crossing of the river, icy and fast through July. Wind southwest through trees to the right of grassy Sanford Park and near 6.0 miles come to the signed junction with the High Meadow Trail. Fork right for the hike to Cliff and High Meadow Lake; climb steadily west and north through switchbacks and pass good lookouts of the broad Sanford Park grasslands. Shadowed canyons amid a broad granite range show beyond, highest around 13,400-foot Wind River Peak at 187°/SSW. Cross a tiny tributary, resume a climb as High Meadow Creek shows briefly left, then break over one ridge, and then another. As the hillside levels near a cairn and blazed tree, several trails diverge: Bear west on the main, blazed trail and contour along the north valleyside. Pass a fork left to a lake in view through the pine near mile 8.0, eventually begin a downhill traverse past a pond (left), then cross a tributary and a marsh and High Meadow Creek. Climb between High Meadow Creek (right) and another tributary (left) and soon fork left to Cliff Lake at 8.8 miles. Another spur trail bends right, makes a steep climb through limber pine, and reaches the south shore of High Meadow Lake at 8.9 miles.

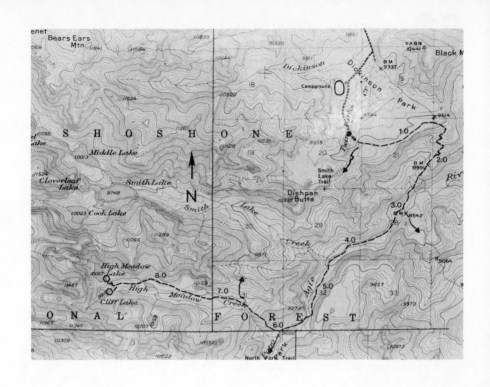

National Outdoor Leadership School meeting

61

LONESOME LAKE VIA THE NORTH FORK TRAIL

Backpack
Distances:
High Meadow Trail - 6.0 miles/9.7 KM.
  Pinto Park Trail - 8.0 miles/12.8 KM.
  Lizard Head Trail - 13.0 miles/20.9 KM.
  Lonesome Lake - 15.0 miles/24.1 KM.
Hiking time: 9-9½ hours one way
Elevation gain: 2,000 feet/610 M.
Elevation loss: 1,215 feet/370 M.
Maximum elevation: 10,185 feet/3,104 M.
Season: Mid-July through mid-September
Topographic map:
  U.S.G.S. Moccasin Lake, Wyo. 1937*
  ***15 minute series**
Lander Ranger District
Shoshone National Forest

Steep, glaciated spires and cliffs, known collectively as the Cirque of the Towers, surround Lonesome Lake in a stunning display of geologic grandeur. This rugged amphitheatre makes an excellent destination for a one-day trip from base camp, perhaps from Valentine Lake via Lizard Head Trail (No's 62 and 63) or along the North Fork Popo Agie River or near pristine Big Basin Lake. Although the North Fork Trail measures about 15 miles in contrast to the Big Sandy Trail/Jackass Pass route (No. 50) or 10.2 miles, its gentler climb and more scenic setting make it the recommended access. Be very careful of the river crossings, especially the third at mile 7.7; in July consider the use trail north of the river. Do not camp at Lonesome Lake.

Turn west from U.S. 287 north of Lander and proceed on the Moccasin Lake Road to the North Fork and Smith Lake Trailhead, following the directions given for No. 59.

Follow the North Fork Trail from Twin Parks Creek up the North Fork Popo Agie Valley to the High Meadow Trail turnoff near 6.0 miles, as described in Cliff and High Meadows Lakes (No. 60). To proceed to Lonesome Lake, stay left on the North Fork Trail, cross High Meadow Creek in another 50 years, and wind past several campsites. Continue inside treeline as the valleysides crowds in from the right after mile 6.5 and as scattered conifers mark the end of Sanford Park (left). Swing left at 7.7 miles to a third crossing of the North Fork Popo Agie River, **in July usually too dangerous to attempt without safety ropes,** and climb steadily through two switchbacks to

the Pinto Park Trail turnoff at mile 8.0, the link with Deep Creek and Ice Lakes, and Tayo Park (No's 58, 57, and 56). Stay right, cross a series of three creeks which drain the valley below Hidden Lake, and pass parks in view across the river north.

Eventually skirt a small talus field (left) where a screened view opens at 277°/WNW of the rock range behind Sheep Lake. Near 9.4 miles bend slightly left and soon make the fourth crossing of the North Fork, then climb gradually west to a crossing over two tributaries from Sheep Lake. As the trail contours farther up the valley, the panorama ahead expands to include an unnamed, 11,250-foot-plus peak at 195°/SSW, then a steep-walled bowl right, and a massive 11,759-foot stone block farther right. Make a short, steep climb after 10.2 miles, heading toward the 11,759-foot mountain wall at 306°/NW. Near 11.1 miles pass the deep talus field at 200°/SW which links the 11,759- and 11,320-foot summits, and at 11.9 miles continue by a prominent pinnacle at 202°/SW, above unseen Big Basin and Basin Lakes and north of Big Sandy Mountain. Enter trees again, cross a small tributary, then cross another and follow along the left side of it. After mile 12.5 pass a shallow pond (left) at the base of magnificent, four-columned Dog Tooth Peak at 210°/SW, soon swing right toward titled Lizard Head Peak at 305°/NW, and break into a clearing at 13.0 miles where the Lizard Head Trail forks right (north, see No. 63).

Fork left for the final leg to Lonesome Lake; drop into Lizard Head Meadows and skirt willows (left), now with an entrancing view of the Cirque of the Towers. Pass a glimpse of a small pond (right), cross the tributary from Bear and East Lizard Head Lakes, and wind past the broad flank of 12,482-foot Mitchell Peak due south. Bend slightly right through open meadows of Indian paintbrush, northwest cinquefoil, elephanthead, and other beautiful wildflowers, cross several tiny tributaries amid stunted willows, limber pine, and Engelmann spruce, and drop to the east shore of Lonesome Lake at mile 15.0. The famous view at this point includes: 12,369-foot Warbonnet Peak at 175°/SSW; pointed, 12,288-feet Watchtower Peak at 237°/WSW; 11,884-foot Pingora (meaning "rocky inaccessible tower" in Shoshone) pinnacle at 264°/W in front of precipitous Sharks Nose, Wolfs Head, and 12,232-foot Bollinger Peak.

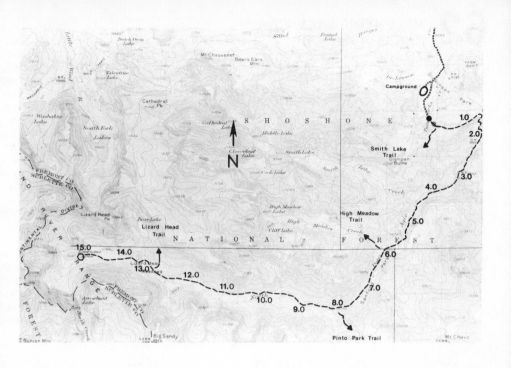

Cirque of the Towers from Lizard Head Meadows

62 VALENTINE LAKE VIA THE BEARS EARS TRAIL

Backpack
Distances:
  Lizard Head Trail - 9.2 miles/14.8 KM.
  Moss Lake Trail - 11.7 miles/18.8 KM.
  Valentine Lake - 12.1 miles/19.5 KM.
Hiking time: 7-8 hours one way
Elevation gain: 3,050 feet/930 M.
Elevation loss: 2,000 feet/610 M.
Maximum elevation: 11,950 feet/3,642 M.
Season: Early July through September
Topographic map:
  U.S.G.S. Moccasin Lake, Wyo. 1937*
    *15 minute series
Lander Ranger District
Shoshone National Forest

A sea of blue, snow-streaked pinnacles and spires unfolds in magnificent splendor along the western skyline near the end of the Bears Ears Trail. This awe-inspiring vista, indeed one of the most memorable in the Wind River Range, plus excellent fishing conditions in the many lakes beneath the peaktops, mark the highlights for the trip, just reward for the arduous, sometimes monotonous access. Begin early and with good weather to be able to cross the open, alpine flats and reach sheltered campsites near Valentine, Upper Valentine, or Dutch Oven Lakes (see No. 64) in one day. Or turn north at mile 5.6 and bivouac among the few trees around Bears Ears Lake, also called Rainbow Lake by some, and Damn Fool Lake by others "because anybody is a damn fool to hike all the way down there to catch fish." For trip extensions, see South Fork, Washakie, and Grave Lakes (No's. 63 and 64).

Turn west from U.S. 287 north of Lander onto the Moccasin Lake Road and proceed for 19.8 miles to the Dickinson Park turnoff, as described for Smith Lake, etc. (No. 59). Fork left from the Moccasin Lake Road, continue south for another 1.7 miles to the Bears Ears Trailhead turnoff, and turn right (west). Pass the public corrals (right) and Dickinson Park Station (left) and after 0.6 mile come to a small parking area near the Bears Ears Trailhead.

Hike west-southwest on the double-tracked trail, following a buck fence (right). Wind through limber pine clumps past the meadow south of Ranger Creek and after 0.2 mile begin the first of many miles of switchbacks, more than are indicated on the map photo. Climb through switchbacks above a tributary basin to Funnel Creek, begin another switchbacking climb above South Funnel Creek (right) after 2.5 miles, then curve right (north) around this willow basin near 3.5 miles and soon pass a view of Funnel Lake at 33°/NE. Come to a sign reading "Bears Ears" where the double-pronged outcropping shows at 200°/SW, contour left through a basin and reach the slight saddle of Adams Pass at 4.8 miles. Drop through switchbacks to a basin where Sand Lake can be seen at 27°/NE, eventually cross 100 yards of corduroy over a marsh; proceed through rocky switchbacks between permanent snowfields, and soon cross Sand Creek, the 5.6 mile mark. At this point, by bearing northeast then north through a saddle, a side-trip to Bears Ears Lake is possible, a distance of 0.8 mile from Bears Ears Trail.

To continue on the Bears Ears Trail, head west along the right valleyside of Sand Creek, passing the rock columns and chimneys of Bears Ears Mountain south. Proceed by a sign marking Mt. Chauvenet at 6.4 miles as this rolling, alpine summit shows at 207°/SW, next to another, 12,068-foot high point, fringed with rock columns, at 152°/SSW. After climbing to the right of another snowfield, begin a slow curve to a southerly bearing and soon gain the first vantage of magnificent, jutting Wind River Peaks which form the Continental Divide west. In glacial cirques amid these shadowed spires, alpine lakes glisten in the sun: above-timberline Macon Lake at 240°/WSW; Washakie Lake below and partially-blocked oblong Lock Laven Lake at 252°/W. Bear south over the rocky trail around a ridge (left), cross through a saddle at mile 9.0, then drop through switchbacks and cross a bench to a signed junction with the Lizard Head Trail at 9.2 miles. Fork right (west) away from the deep chasm (east) which leads to Cathedral Lake. Drop gradually along the north valleyside of Valentine Creek, pass a glimpse of a lake (left) at mile 10.0, and descend through a long series of switchbacks. For Valentine Creek and the lake tributaries, pass through Valentine Meadows, then stay left at the Moss Lake Trail junction at 11.7 miles and drop through pine to the north side of Valentine Lake at mile 12.1.

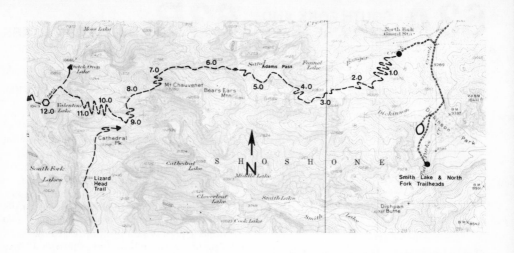

Wind River Range from Bears Ears Trail

63A SOUTH FORK AND WASHAKIE LAKES   63B SOUTH FORK LAKES

Backpack
Hiking time: 9-10 hours one way
Maximum elevation: 11,950 feet/3,642 M.
Season: Mid-July through mid-September
Topographic map:
  U.S.G.S. Moccasin Lake, Wyo. 1937*
    *15 minute series
Lander Ranger District
Shoshone National Forest

Windy, mile-long Upper South Fork Lake rates currently as the hottest fishing spot in the north end of the Popo Agie Wilderness. And since the 1937 U.S.G.S. topo shows no trail to this lake or to Lower South Fork Lake, both are often bypassed by backpackers. Scenic Washakie Lake, which opens to a view of massive, 12,524-foot Mt. Washakie, receives more traffic because of the nearby Washakie Trail, the link with trails to Little Divide Lake (No. 48) and Francis Lake (No. 49) in the Bridger Wilderness. FISH: See Grave Lake (No. 64).

Besides the Bears Ear Tril, another access to Valentine Lake (and on to South Fork, Washakie, and Grave Lakes) is by way of the North Fork Trail to Lizard Head Meadows (see No's. 60 and 61) and then over the Lizard Head Trail to the Bears Ears Trail east of Valentine Lake. This latter trail begins with leg-burning switchbacks up the mountainside east of Bear and East Lizard Head Lakes and traverses the high, rock-strewn range above the east of the South Fork Lakes basin. Since most of the 7-mile-plus distance lies above timberline where protection from wind and rain is scarce, a half-day of good weather is required for the trip. But the exhilaration of traveling through alpine country and the view — of Bear Lake and Lizard Head Peak, of South Fork Glacier, Big Chief Mountain, Mt. Lander, and of countless summits beyond — make this the authors' favorite trail in the Wind River Range.

Drive to the Bears Ears Trailhead, following the instructions for Smith Lake (No. 59) and for Valentine Lake (No. 62).

Distance: (from Bears Ears Trailhead)
  Upper South Fork Lake - 14.8 miles/23.8 KM.
Elevation gain: 3,675 feet/1,120 M.
Elevation loss: 2,505 feet/764 M.

Hike west on the Bears Ears Trail for about 11.7 miles to the Moss Lake Trail junction — marked by a sign reading "Dutch Oven Lake ½ Mile" — northeast of Valentine Lake, as given in No. 62. Fork left, pass Valentine Lake (left) after 12.0 miles, then wind west over the ridge and switchback down into the basin around Upper Valentine Creek at mile 13.0. To get to the South Fork Lakes turn south on a cross-country route where the trail to Washakie and Grave Lake bears west across a wide park. Keep Upper Valentine Creek left and the ridge right and make a mile-long climb at 140°/SSE to a hilltop viewpoint of Lower South Fork Lake (ahead right). Maintain elevation southwest for another mile, then turn toward the looming, 1,000-foot pinnacle of Lizard Head Peak which rises above white South Fork Glacier, and contour through wind-blown conifers to the north shore of Upper South Fork Lake at 14.8 miles.

63C WASHAKIE LAKE

Distance: (from Bears Ears Trailhead)
  Washakie Lake - 14.6 miles/23.5 KM.
Elevation gain: 2,590 feet/789 M.
Elevation loss: 2,575 feet/785 M.

Continue across the Upper Valentine Creek basin at 13.0 miles, drop right toward the South Fork Little Wind River and make a careful crossing at mile 13.2. Turn south on the Washakie Trail as the trail to Grave Lake bears north (see No. 64). Cross a tributary after 200 yards, bear to the right of the giant pillar and walled cliffs that comprise Big Chief Mountain at 147°/SSE, then make a short climb into trees and cross other tributaries. Swing left across Lock Laven Creek at mile

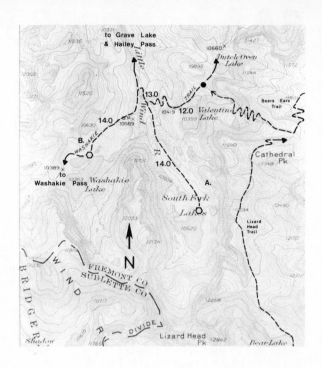

Wilderness ranger

14.0, bear 210°/SW toward the lofty summit of Mt. Washakie, and continue across a hillside of low-lying willows and stunted evergreens to the north side of Washakie Lake at 14.6 miles.

A sign marks the turnoff to Lock Laven Lake, and farther down the trail another sign indicates majestic 12,524-foot Mt. Washakie, here in view at 215°/SW.

64 GRAVE LAKE

Backpack
Distance: (from Bears Ears Trailhead)
Grave Lake - 15.7 miles/25.3 KM.
Hiking time: 10-11 hours one way
Elevation gain: 3,485 feet/1,062 M.
Elevation loss: 2,870 feet/875 M.
Maximum elevation: 11,950 feet/3,642 M.
Season: Early July through mid-September
Topographic map:
U.S.G.S. Moccasin Lake, Wyo. 1937*
***15 minute series**
Lander Ranger District
Shoshone National Forest

Shadowed Grave Lake (named for the Indian grave near the north shore) fills the quiet, northern corner of the Popo Agie Wilderness, immediately south of the Wind River Indian Reservation. For week-long trips, this extremely beautiful, shimmering crescent makes the ultimate destination, reached from the Scab Creek or Big Sandy Entrances (No's. 48 and 49) via Hailey Pass or from the Bears Ears Trailhead, as described below. FISH: Mcknw 18'', Ct in Grave Lake; Brk, Ct in Moss and Bears Ears Lakes; Brk in Dutch Oven, Macon, Sand, and Funnel Lakes; Ct, Gdn, X's in Valentine Lake, Gdn 14'' (pure) in Upper Valentine Lake; Gdn, Rbw in Washakie Lake; Brn, Rbw in Lock Laven Lake; none in Pass Lake.

Drive to the Bears Ears Trailhead, following the instructions for Smith Lake (No. 59) and for Valentine Lake (No. 62).

From the Bears Ears Trailhead hike west for 11.7 miles to the Moss Lake Trail junction — marked by a sign reading "Dutch Oven Lake ½ Mile" — as described in No. 62. Stay left where the Moss Lake Trail, an alternate route to Grave Lake (see below), angles right. Drop through pine past Valentine Lake (left) after 12.0 miles, soon cross the outlet, then wind from southwest to north over a ridge and descend gradually toward a splendid view of solid-rock Wind River Peaks. After 12.6 miles begin long switchbacks to the basin around Upper Valentine Creek, bear west across a wide park which marks the turnoff to South Fork Lakes (see No. 63), and pass viewpoints of massive Big Chief Mountain — the range between the South Fork and Washakie Lakes — at 176°/S. Bend right off the plateau toward the South Fork Little Wind River at mile 13.1 and come to a crossing downstream, **usually**

too swift, deep and cold to attempt in July.

After the crossing head downstream away from towering Big Chief Mountain as the Washakie Trail to Washakie Lake (No. 63) proceeds upstream. Follow the level trail north through stunted willows on the left valleyside, enter a narrower valley near 13.7 miles, then bend at 317°/NNW toward a saddle above Raft Creek and proceed through conifers to a trail junction at mile 14.5. Fork left onto the Grave Lake/Hailey Pass trail where the Moss Lake Trail loops across the South Fork (right). In 20 yards ford a tributary from lakes southwest, turn left at three blazes and climb steadily upstream, soon passing cascades (left). Wind north and west through scenic, open limber pine with a carpet of whortleberry for ground cover; follow the hillside contour on a bend right and pass above a pond farther right at 15.2 miles. Make a winding drop northwest, cross a tributary at mile 15.4 from another lake southwest, and traverse past a basin (right) and over a slight rise to the east side of Grave Lake, about 15.7 miles from the Bears Ears Trailhead. Here the vista opens to include a sheer-rock, tombstone-shaped wall at 262°/W which rises to the 10,818-foot summit. Rock pillars mark Petroleum Peak at 277°/WNW beyond, and the forested, rock-topped 11,226-foot summit at 293°/NW drops right into the canyon of Grave Creek.

To make the highly recommended loop past Moss and Dutch Oven Lakes, fork right back at mile 14.5 across the South Fork Little Wind River. Follow blazes on a mile-long, winding climb to the north side of Valentine Mountain, passing splendid viewpoints of Grave Lake and the snow-streaked range beyond. Eventually bear east along a solid granite corridor (right), drop to a tributary of Moss Creek, and contour southwest into conifers. Stay left where the trail to Gaylord Lake, an enticing alternate route, forks east across Moss Creek north of Moss Lake. After a sidetrip south to Moss Lake and perhaps to Little Moss Lake farther east, continue the loop with a steep climb southwest above Moss Creek (left), cross glacier-polished rock hillsides (right), and follow the Moss Creek headwaters to an alpine flat where the view again scans high peaks west. Proceed across the outlet from Dutch Oven Lake (left) and bear southwest through a small saddle to end the loop at the Bears Ears Trail junction northeast of Valentine Lake.

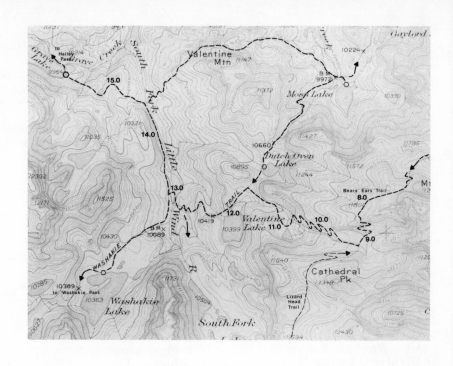

Tree skeletons at Grave Lake

Index

All references listed below are to the pages, rather than to the hike number. In the case of identical names, the source valley or creek is indicated also. Abbreviations include Cmpgrd for Campground, Cr for Creek, E for East, Entr for Entrance, Fk for Fork, Mt for Mount, Mtn for Mountain, No for North, Pk for Peak, Rd for Road, So for South, Tr for Trail, Trhd for Trailhead, W for West.

Lakes are followed by the fish specie(s) therein, if known, listed in parentheses. Many lakes, not mentioned in the text, are indexed below to provide fish information. Abbreviations include Brk for brook trout, Brn for brown trout, Ct for native cutthroat trout, Gdn for golden trout, Mcknw for mackinaw trout, and Rbw for Rainbow trout (see WILDLIFE AND FISH).